# American
# Bureaucracy

*Trans*-action Books

# American Bureaucracy

*Edited by*
WARREN G. BENNIS

*Trans-* **action** Books

Published by
Aldine Publishing Company

The essays in this book originally appeared
in *Trans-* **action** Magazine

TA Book 14
Library of Congress Catalog Number 73-115-943

# Contents

# Preface

However diverse their attitudes and interpretations may sometimes be, social scientists are now entering a period of shared realization that the United States—both at home and abroad—has entered a crucial period of transition. Indeed, the much burdened word "crisis" has now become a commonplace among black militants, Wall Street lawyers, housewives, and even professional politicians.

For the past seven years, *Trans*-action magazine has dedicated itself to the task of reporting the strains and conflicts within the American system. But the magazine has done more than this. It has pioneered in social programs for changing the society, offered the kind of analysis that has permanently restructured the terms of the "dialogue" between peoples and publics, and offered the sort of prognosis that makes for real alterations in social and political policies directly affecting our lives.

The work done in the pages of *Trans*-action has crossed

professional boundaries. This represents much more than simple cross-disciplinary "team efforts." It embodies rather a recognition that the social world cannot be easily carved into neat academic areas. That, indeed, the study of the experience of blacks in American ghettos, or the manifold uses and abuses of agencies of law enforcement, or the sorts of overseas policies that lead to the celebration of some dictatorships and the condemnation of others, can best be examined from many viewpoints and from the vantage points of many disciplines.

This series of books clearly demonstrates the superiority of starting with real world problems and searching out practical solutions, over the zealous guardianship of professional boundaries. Indeed, it is precisely this approach that has elicited enthusiastic support from leading American social scientists for this new and dynamic series of books.

The demands upon scholarship and scientific judgment are particularly stringent, for no one has been untouched by the current situation. Each essay republished in these volumes bears the imprint of the author's attempt to communicate his own experience of the crisis. Yet, despite the sense of urgency these papers exhibit, the editors feel that many have withstood the test of time, and match in durable interest the best of available social science literature. This collection of *Trans*-action articles, then, attempts to address itself to immediate issues without violating the basic insights derived from the classical literature in the various fields of social science.

The subject matter of these books concern social changes that have aroused the long-standing needs and present-day anxieties of us all. These changes are in organizational life styles, concepts of human ability and intelligence, changing patterns of norms and morals, the relationship of social conditions to physical and biological environments, and in the status of social science with national policy making.

The dissident minorities, massive shifts in norms of social conduct, population explosions and urban expansions, and vast realignments between nations of the world of recent years do not promise to disappear in the seventies. But the social scientists involved as editors and authors of this *Trans*-action series have gone beyond observation of these critical areas, and have entered into the vital and difficult tasks of explanation and interpretation. They have defined issues in a way making solutions possible. They have provided answers as well as asked the right questions. Thus, this series should be conceived as the first collection dedicated not to hightlighting social problems alone, but to establishing guidelines for social solutions based on the social sciences.

THE EDITORS
*Trans*-action

# *Introduction*

WARREN G. BENNIS

Corsica, according to Gibbon, is easier to deplore than describe. The same holds for "bureaucracy," I suppose, which is strange indeed as very few of us have lived in Corsica, but all of us have lived in bureaucracies—for many years. Bureaucracy is a term invented by Max Weber to analyze the pervasive pyramidal form of human effort, as old as time itself. Since I attempt a brief definition in the first essay, I won't belabor definitional problems now, except to say that I use "organization" and "bureaucracy" as synonyms for convenience, and throughout the book, this convention seems to hold up rather well. I should also say, by way of introduction, that the mystique and ambiguity emanating from bureaucracy can only be explained, in my view, in the same context as the old proverb, "Fish discover water the last."

As to its importance, nobody will argue. We are all "organization men and women," like it or not. Contem-

1

porary man is "man-in-organization." We spend the majority of our waking hours in a bureaucracy; we establish an identity and status in a bureaucracy; we seem to garner most of our satisfactions and disappointments in a bureaucracy. Increasingly, what a man *is* relates to what he does.

Aside from the importance of understanding those institutions which shape our values, behavior and experience—our lives—the study of bureaucracy is a vital area for the social sciences, for it "overtualizes" the recalcitrant and underlying problems of society in a compact and comprehensible way. These problems, too abstract and ephemeral in society, are here down to earth: measureable, comprehensible, visible in the microcosm, bureaucracy. Problems of power and influence, change, innovation and resistances to change and innovation, intergroup conflict, ambition and aspiration, self-realization versus organizational goals (such as efficiency), expertise versus participative democracy, technology versus humanism: all of these problems can be observed and felt in human organizations.

In this book of readings, all taken from *Trans*-action, the articles are written in clear and simple English, devoid of jargon. They also tend to stop after their points are made, a refreshing change from typical academic writing, which usually begins after the point is made. Rather than repeat myself later, I suggest that the reader turn to the last essay in the book for my appraisal of the major implications of these articles—for the individual, the family, society, and institutional life.

# Beyond Bureaucracy

WARREN G. BENNIS

Most of us spend all of our working day and a great deal of our non-working day in a unique and extremely durable social arrangement called "bureaucracy." I use the term "bureaucracy" descriptively, not as an epithet about those "guys in Washington" or as a metaphor *a la* Kafka's *Castle* which conjures up an image of red tape, or faceless and despairing masses standing in endless lines. Bureaucracy, as I shall use the term here, is a social invention, perfected during the industrial revolution to organize and direct the activities of the business firm.

It is my premise that the bureaucratic form of organization is becoming less and less effective; that it is hopelessly out of joint with contemporary realities; that new shapes, patterns, and models are emerging which promise drastic changes in the conduct of the corporation and of managerial practices in general. In the next 25 to 50 years we should witness, and participate in, the end of bureaucracy and the

3

rise of new social systems better suited to twentieth century demands of industrialization. (Sociological evolutionists substantially agree that 25 to 50 years from now most people in the world will live in industrialized societies.)

Corsica, according to Gibbon, is much easier to deplore than to describe. The same holds true for bureaucracy. Basically, bureaucracy is a social invention which relies exclusively on the power to influence through rules, reason, and law. Max Weber, the German sociologist who developed the theory of bureaucracy around the turn of the century, once described bureaucracy as a social machine:

> Bureaucracy is like a modern judge who is a vending machine into which the pleadings are inserted together with the fee and which then disgorges the judgment together with its reasons mechanically derived from the code.

The bureaucratic "machine model" Weber outlined was developed as a reaction against the personal subjugation, nepotism, cruelty, emotional vicissitudes, and capricious judgment which passed for managerial practices in the early days of the industrial revolution. The true hope for man, it was thought, lay in his ability to rationalize, calculate, to use his head as well as his hands and heart. Thus, in the bureaucratic system social roles were institutionalized and reinforced by legal tradition rather than by the "cult of personality"; rationality and predictability were sought for in order to eliminate chaos and unanticipated consequences; emphasis was placed on technical competence rather than arbitrary or "iron whims." These are oversimplifications, to be sure, but contemporary analysts of organizations would tend to agree with them. In fact, there is a general consensus that the anatomy of bureaucracy consists of the following "organs":

■ a division of labor based on functional specialization.

■ a well-defined hierarchy of authority.
■ a system of rules covering the rights and duties of employees.
■ a system of procedures for dealing with work situations.
■ impersonality of interpersonal relations.
■ promotion and selection based on technical competence.

It does not take great critical imagination to detect the flaws and problems in the bureaucratic model. We have all *experienced* them:

■ bosses without (and underlings with) technical competence.
■ arbitrary and zany rules.
■ an underworld (or informal) organization which subverts or even replaces the formal apparatus.
■ confusion and conflict among roles.
■ cruel treatment of subordinates based not on rational or legal grounds but upon inhumanity.

The tremendous range of unanticipated consequences provides a gold mine of material for comics like Charlie Chaplin and Jacques Tati who capture with a smile or a shrug the absurdity of authority systems based on pseudologic and inappropriate rules.

Almost everybody, including many observers of organizational behavior, approaches bureaucracy with a chip on his shoulder. It has been attacked for many reasons: for theoretical confusion and contradictions; for moral and ethical reasons; on practical grounds such as its inefficiency; for methodological weaknesses; for containing too many implicit values and for containing too few. I have recently catalogued the criticisms of bureaucracy and they outnumber and outdo the ninety-five theses tacked on the church door at Wittenberg in attacking another bureaucracy. A small sample of these:

(1) Bureaucracy does not adequately allow for personal

growth and the development of mature personalities.

(2) It develops conformity and "group-think."

(3) It does not take into account the "informal organization" and the emergent and unanticipated problems.

(4) Its systems of control and authority are hopelessly outdated.

(5) It has no adequate juridical process.

(6) It does not possess adequate means for resolving differences and conflicts between ranks, and most particularly, between functional groups.

(7) Communication (and innovative ideas) are thwarted or distorted due to hierarchical divisions.

(8) The full human resources of bureaucracy are not being utilized due to mistrust, fear of reprisals, etc.

(9) It cannot assimilate the influx of new technology or scientists entering the organization.

(10) It modifies personality structure so that people become and reflect the dull, gray, conditioned "organization man."

Max Weber, the developer of the theory of bureaucracy, came around to condemn the apparatus he helped immortalize. While he felt that bureaucracy was inescapable, he also thought it might strangle the spirit of capitalism or the entrepreneurial attitude, a theme which Schumpeter later developed. And in a debate on bureaucracy Weber once said, more in sorrow than in anger:

It is horrible to think that the world could one day be filled with nothing but those little cogs, little men clinging to little jobs and striving towards bigger ones—a state of affairs which is to be seen once more, as in the Egyptian records, playing an ever-increasing part in the spirit of our present administrative system, and especially of its offspring, the students. This passion for bureaucracy . . . is enough to drive one to despair. It is as if in politics . . . we were deliberately to become men who need 'order' and nothing but order, who become nervous and cowardly if for one moment this order wavers, and helpless if they are torn away from their total incorporation in it. That the world should know no men but these: it is such an evolution that we are already caught up in, and the great question is therefore not how we can promote and hasten it, but what can we oppose to this machinery in order to keep a portion of mankind free from this parcelling-out of the soul, from this supreme mastery of the bureaucratic way of life.

In what ways has bureaucracy been modified over the years in order to cope more successfully with the problems that beset it? Before answering that, we have to say something about the nature of organizations, *all* organizations, from mass production leviathans all the way to service industries such as the university or hospital. Organizations are primarily complex, goal-seeking units. In order to survive they must also accomplish the secondary tasks of (1) maintaining their internal system and co-ordinating the "human side of enterprise"—a process of mutual compliance here called *reciprocity*—and (2) adapting to and shaping the external environment—here called *adaptability*. These two organizational dilemmas can help us to organize the pivotal ways in which the bureaucratic mechanism has been altered—and found wanting.

Reciprocity primarily covers the processes which can mediate conflict between the goals of management and the individual goals of the workers. Over the past several decades a number of interesting theoretical and practical resolutions have been made which truly allow for conflict and mediation of interest. They revise, if not transform, the very nature of the bureaucratic mechanism by explicit recognition of the inescapable tension between individual and organizational goals. These theories can be called, variously, *exchange, group, value, structural, situational*—depending on what variable of the situation one wishes to modify.

The *exchange* theories postulate that wages, incomes, and services are given to the individual for an equal contribution to the organization in work. If the inducements are not adequate, men may withdraw and work elsewhere. This may be elaborated upon by regarding "payments" to individuals as including motivational units. That is to say, the organization provides a psychological anchor in times of rapid social change and a hedge against personal loss, as well as position, growth and mastery, success experience, and so forth—in exchange for energy, work, commitment.

Management tends to interpret motivation in economic terms. Man is logical; man acts in the manner which serves his self-interest; man is competitive. Elton Mayo and his associates were among the first to see human *affiliation* as a motivating force, to view industrial organization as a *social* system as well as an economic-technical system. A manager, they stated, should be judged in terms of his ability to sustain co-operation. In fact, once a cohesive, primary work group is seen as a motivating force, a managerial elite may become obsolete, and the work group itself becomes the decision maker. This allows decisions to be made at the most relevant point of the organization, where the data are most available.

Before this becomes possible, however, some theorists believe that the impersonal *value* system of bureaucracy must be modified. In this case the manager plays an important role as the instrument of change in interpersonal relations. He must instill values which permit and reinforce the expression of feeling, experimentalism, and norms of individuality, trust, and concern. Management, according to R. R. Blake, is successful insofar as it maximizes a "concern for people"—with "concern for production."

Others believe that a new conception of the *structure* of bureaucracy will create more relevant attitudes towards the function of management than formal role specifications now do. If the organization is seen as organic rather than mechanistic, as adapting spontaneously to its needs, then decisions will be made at the critical point and roles and jobs will devolve on the "natural" organizational incumbent. The shift would probably be from the individual level to cooperative group effort, from delegated to shared responsibility, from centralized to decentralized authority, from obedience to confidence, from antagonistic arbitration to problem-solving. Management centered upon problem-solving, that assumes or relaxes authority according to task demands, has most concerned some theorists who are as much interested in an organization's success and productivity as in its social system.

However, on all sides we find a growing belief that the effectiveness of bureaucracy should be evaluated by human *situation* as well as economic criteria. Social satisfaction and personal growth of employees must be considered as well as the productivity and profit of the organization. The criticism and revisions of the bureaucratic organization tend to concentrate on the internal system and its human components. But although it appears on the surface that the case against bureaucracy has to do with its ethical-moral posture and the social fabric, the real *coup de grace* has come from the environment.

Bureaucracy thrives in a highly competitive, undifferentiated and stable environment, such as the climate of its youth, the Industrial Revolution. A pyramidal structure of authority, with power concentrated in the hands of a few with the knowledge and resources to control an entire enterprise was, and is, an eminently suitable social arrangement for routinized tasks.

However, the environment has changed in just those ways which make the mechanism most problematic. Stability has vanished. As Ellis Johnson said, ". . . the once-reliable constants have now become galloping variables."

The factors accelerating change include:

■ the growth of science, research and development activities, and intellectual technology.

■ the increase of transactions with social institutions (and their importance in conducting the enterprise)—including government, distributors and consumers, shareholders, competitors, raw material and power suppliers, sources of employees (particularly managers), trade unions, and groups within the firms. There is also more interdependence between the economic and other facets of society, leading to greater complications of legislation and public regulation.

■ competition between firms diminishing as their fates interwine and become positively correlated.

My argument so far, to summarize quickly, is that the first assault on bureaucracy arose from its incapacity to manage the tension between individual and management goals. However, this conflict is somewhat mediated by the growth of a new ethic of productivity which includes personal growth and/or satisfaction. The second and more major shock to bureaucracy is caused by the scientific and technological revolution. It is the requirement of *adaptability* to the environment which leads to the predicted demise of bureaucracy and to the collapse of management as we know it now.

A forecast falls somewhere between a prediction and a prophecy. It lacks the divine guidance of the latter and the empirical foundation of the former. On thin empirical ice, I want to set forth some of the conditions that will dictate organizational life in the next 25 to 50 years.

■ THE ENVIRONMENT. Those factors already mentioned will continue in force and increase. Rapid technological change and diversification will lead to interpenetration of the government—its legal and economic policies—with business. Partnerships between industry and government (like Telstar) will be typical. And because of the immensity and expense of the projects, there will be fewer identical units competing for the same buyers and sellers. Or, in reverse, imperfect competition leads to an oligopolistic and government-business controlled economy. The three main features of the environment will be (1) interdependence rather than competition, (2) turbulence rather than steadiness, and (3) large scale rather than small enterprises.

■ POPULATION CHARACTERISTICS. We are living in what Peter Drucker calls the "educated society," and I think this is the most distinctive characteristic of our times. Within fifteen years, two-thirds of our population living in metropolitan areas will have attended college. Adult education programs, especially the management development courses of such universities as M.I.T., Harvard, and Stanford, are expanding and adding intellectual breadth. All this, of course, is not just "nice," but necessary. For as Secretary of Labor Wirtz has pointed out, computers can do the work of most high school graduates—cheaper and more effectively. Fifty years ago education used to be regarded as "nonwork" and intellectuals on the payroll (and many of the staff) were considered "overhead." Today, the survival of the firm depends, more than ever before, on the proper exploitation of brain power.

One other characteristic of the population which will aid our understanding of organizations of the future is increasing job mobility. The lowered expense and ease of transportation, coupled with the real needs of a dynamic environment, will change drastically the idea of "owning" a job—or "having roots," for that matter. Participants will be shifted from job to job and even employer to employer with much less fuss than we are accustomed to.

■ WORK VALUES. The increased level of education and mobility will change the values we hold about work. People will be more intellectually committed to their jobs and will probably require more involvement, participation, and autonomy in their work. (This turn of events is due to a composite of the following factors: (1) positive correlation between a person's education and his need for autonomy; (2) job mobility places the educated in a position of greater influence in the system; (3) job requirements call for more responsibility and discretion.)

Also, people will tend to be more "other-directed" in their dealings with others. David McClelland's studies suggest that as industrialization increases, "other-directedness" increases; so we will tend to rely more heavily on temporary social arrangements, on our immediate and constantly-changing colleagues.

■ TASKS AND GOALS. The tasks of the firm will be more technical, complicated, and unprogrammed. They will rely more on the intellect than muscle. And they will be too complicated for one person to handle or for individual supervision. Essentially, they will call for the collaboration of specialists in a project or team form of organization.

Similarly there will be a complication of goals. "Increased profits" and "raised productivity" will sound like oversimplifications and cliches. Business will concern itself increasingly with its adaptive or innovative-creative capacity. In addition, *meta*-goals will have to be articulated and developed; that is, supra-goals which shape and provide the foundation for the goal structure. For example, one meta-goal might be a system for detecting new and changing goals; another could be a system for deciding priorities among goals.

Finally, there will be more conflict and contradiction among diverse standards of organizational effectiveness, just as in hospitals and universities today there is conflict between teaching and research. The reason for this is the increased number of professionals involved, who tend to identify as much with the supra-goals of their profession as with those of their immediate employer. University professors can be used as a case in point. More and more of their income comes from outside sources, such as private or public foundations and consultant work. They tend not to make good "company men" because they are divided in their loyalty to professional values and organizational demands.

■ ORGANIZATION. The social structure of organizations of the future will have some unique characteristics. The key word will be "temporary"; there will be adaptive, rapidly changing *temporary systems*. These will be "task forces" organized around problems-to-be-solved. The problems will be solved by groups of relative strangers who represent a set of diverse professional skills. The groups will be arranged on organic rather than mechanical models; they will evolve in response to a problem rather than to programmed role expectations. The "executive" thus becomes a coordinator or "linking pin" between various task forces. He must be a man who can speak the diverse languages of research, with skills to relay information and to mediate between groups. *People will be differentiated not vertically, according to rank and role, but flexibly and functionally according to skill and professional training.*

Adaptive, problem-solving, temporary systems of diverse specialists, linked together by co-ordinating and task evaluating specialists in an organic flux—this is the organizational form that will gradually replace bureaucracy as we know it. As no catchy phrase comes to mind, let us call this an *organic-adaptive* structure.

As an aside—what will happen to the rest of society, to the manual laborers, to the less educated, to those who desire to work under conditions of high authority, and so forth? Many such jobs will disappear; other jobs will be automated. However, there will be a corresponding growth in the service-type occupations, such as those in the "war on poverty" and the Peace Corps programs. In times of change, where there is a discrepancy between cultures, when industrialization and especially urbanization proceeds rapidly, the market for men with training and skill in human interaction increases. We might guess that approximately 40 percent of the population would be involved in jobs of this nature, 40 percent in technological jobs, with a 20 percent bureaucratic minority.

■ MOTIVATION. Our above discussion of "reciprocity" indicated the shortcomings of bureaucracy in maximizing employee effectiveness. The "organic-adaptive" structure should increase motivation, and thereby effectiveness, because it enhances satisfactions intrinsic to the task. There is a harmony between the educated individual's need for meaningful, satisfactory, and creative tasks and a flexible organizational structure.

Of course, where the reciprocity problem is ameliorated, there are corresponding tensions between the individual's involvement in his professional community and his involvement in his employing organization. Professionals are notoriously "disloyal" to organizational demands.

There will, however, also be reduced commitment to

work groups, for these groups, as I have already mentioned, will be transient and changing. While skills in human interaction will become more important, due to the growing needs for collaboration in complex tasks, there will be a concomitant reduction in group cohesiveness. I would predict that in the organic-adaptive system people will have to learn to develop quick and intense relationships on the job, and learn to bear the loss of more enduring work relationships.

In general I do not agree with Clark Kerr, Harold Leavitt, and others in their emphasis on a "New Bohemianism" in which leisure—not work—becomes the emotional-creative sphere of life. They assume a technological slow-down and leveling-off, and a stabilizing of social mobility. This may happen in a society of the distant future. But long before then we will face the challenge of creating the new service-type organizations with an organic-adaptive structure.

Jobs in the next century should become more rather than less involving; man is a problem-solving animal and the tasks of the future guarantee a full agenda of problems. In addition, the adaptive process itself may become captivating to many. At the same time, I think that the future I described is not necessarily a "happy" one. Coping with rapid change, living in the temporary work systems, setting up (in quick-step time) meaningful relations—and then breaking them—all augur social strains and psychological tensions. Learning how to live with ambiguity and to be self-directing will be the task of education and the goal of maturity.

In these new organizations, participants will be called on to use their minds more than at any other time in history. Fantasy, imagination, and creativity will be legitimate in ways that today seem strange. Social structures will no longer be instruments of psychic repression but will increasingly promote play and freedom on behalf of curiosity and thought. I agree with Herbert Marcuse's thesis in *Eros and Civilization* that the necessity of repression and the suffering derived from it, decreases with the maturity of the civilization.

Not only will the problem of adaptability be overcome through the organic-adaptive structure, but the problem we started with, reciprocity, will be resolved. Bureaucracy, with its "surplus repression," was a monumental discovery for harnessing muscle power *via* guilt and instinctual renunciation. In today's world, it is a lifeless crutch that is no longer useful. For we now require structures of freedom to permit the expression of play and imagination and to exploit the new pleasure of work.

*July/August 1965*

# Being Human
# and Being Organized

CHRIS ARGYRIS

It is hard to imagine being "civilized" without being "organized." Yet too much organization or the wrong kind, can injure the individuals involved and through them can spoil an organization or a civilization. How can we design or "grow" organizations that maintain the right balance between individual needs on the one hand, and organizational requirements on the other?

The classical design for a formal organization has some very serious flaws. The nature of these flaws appears when we set two pictures side by side: first, a view of how human beings need to behave in our society in order to be healthy, productive, growing individuals; and second, how a formal organization (a factory, business or hospital) requires them to behave. Comparing these pictures, we see that the organization's requirements, as presented by "classical" descriptions, are sharply opposed to the individual's needs. We can, however, suggest some lines along which action

17

and study might improve the "fit" between the human being and the nonhuman organization.

There are certain lines along which the child becoming a man develops in our culture. We can discuss as being most important seven of these "developmental dimensions:"

- From being passive as infants, humans grow toward activeness as adults.
- From being dependent on others, an individual grows toward being relatively independent of others. He develops the ability to "stand on his own two feet" while at the same time acknowledging a healthy dependency. He does not react to others (his boss, for instance) in terms of patterns learned during childhood; thus, such independence is partly a matter of accurate perception of himself and those around him.
- From only a few types of reaction or behavior, he develops many.
- He moves from the shallow, brief and erratic interests of his infancy to the intense, long-term and coherent commitments of adulthood. He requires increasingly varied challenges; he wants his tasks to be not easy but hard, not simple but complex, not a collection of separate things but a variety of parts he can put together.
- He begins to want long-term challenges that link his part and future in place of the old brief and unconnected jobs which typically he engaged in as a child.
- He begins wanting to go up the totem pole instead of staying in the low place a child has.
- He develops from being not very self-aware and impulsive to being both self-aware and self-controlled, and this lets him develop a sense of integrity and self-worth.

No one, of course, finishes his development along these

seven lines. For one thing, if everyone became totally independent, incessantly active and completely equal if not superior, society would be in a pretty difficult situation—sort of all fleas and no dog. One function of culture is to hold back, by our manners and morals, the self-expression of some individualists, so that others may also have a chance at self-development. Then too, people simply differ in needs and skills; not everybody wants to go into orbit, and some are too frail, too fat or too stupid to be given the chance.

Admitting, then, that no one is ever through developing along these dimensions, we can still say that his self-actualization is the overall "profile" of how far he has developed along them. At this point we must add that in drawing this profile, not the surface appearance but the underlying meanings of a man's behavior are what have to be considered. For instance, an employee might seem to be always going against what management wants, so that people call him "independent," yet his contrariness may be due to his great need to be dependent on management, a need he dislikes to admit. The truly independent person is the one whose behavior is not mainly a reaction against the influence others have over him (though, of course, no person is totally independent). The best test of such independence is how fully the person will let other people be independent and active. Autocratic leaders may claim to like independent underlings, yet many studies have shown that autocratic leadership only makes both boss and underlings more dependence-ridden.

We turn now from the picture of a developing self to the organization. What are its properties, and what impact can we expect these to make on the human personality we have just viewed? What reactions can we expect from this impact?

To begin, the most basic feature of a formal organization is that it is "rational"—that is, it has been designed, and its parts are purposefully related within this design; it has pattern and is shaped by human minds to accomplish particular rational objectives. For instance, jobs within it must be clearly defined (in terms of rank, salary and duties) so that the organization can have logical training, promotion and resignation or retirement policies.

But most experts on such organizations are not content to point to this rational design, as Herbert Simon does—they go on to say that this rationality, though an ideal that may have to be modified now and then, requires people in an organization to be very loyal to its formal structure if it is to work effectively. They have to go by the rules. And the experts claim such design is "more human" in the long run than creating an organization haphazardly. It is senseless, cruel, wasteful and inefficient, they argue, not to have a logical design. It is senseless to pay a man highly without clearly defining his position and its relation to the whole. It is cruel, because eventually people suffer when no structure exists. It is wasteful because without clearly predefined jobs it is impossible to plan a logical training or promotion or resignation or retirement policy. And it is inefficient because it allows the personal touch to dominate and this, in turn, is playing politics.

In contrast to such experts, some human-relations researchers have unfortunately given the impression that formal structures are bad, and that individual needs should come first in creating and running an organization. These latter men, however, are beginning (as recent analysis of their research has shown) to recognize that an extreme emphasis on the individual's needs is not a very tenable position either, and that organizational rules can be well worth keeping.

What are the principles by which an organization is rationally designed? The traditionalists among experts in this field have singled out certain key assumptions about the best design for a formal organization. In our comments here these will be dealt with not as beyond question but only as the most useful and accurate so far offered. By accepting them to this extent, we can go on to look at the probable impact on human beings of an organization based on them.

As Gillespie suggests, these principles may be traced back to certain "principles of industrial economics," the most important of which is that "the concentration of effort on a limited field of endeavor increases quality and quantity of output." This principle leads to another: that the more similar the things that need doing, the more specialization will help to do them.

The design-principle just mentioned carries three implications about human beings within organizations. First, that the human personality will behave more efficiently as the job gets more specialized. Second, that there can be found a one best way to define the job so it will be done faster. Third, that differences between human personalities may be ignored by transferring more skill and thought to machines.

But all these assumptions conflict sharply with the developmental needs or tendencies of human personality as a growing thing; a human being is always putting himself together, pushing himself into the future. How can we assume that this process can be choked off, or that the differences between individuals which result from the process can be ignored?

Besides, specialization requires a person to use only a few of his abilities, and the more specialized the task the simpler the ability involved. This goes directly counter to the human tendency to want more complex, more interesting jobs as he develops. Singing the same tune over and over is boring enough, but repeating the same note is absolutely maddening.

Mere efficiency of parts is not enough; an organization needs to have a pattern of parts, a chain of command. Thus, planners create "leadership," to control and coordinate. They assume that efficiency is increased by a fixed hierarchy of authority. The man at the top is given formal power to hire and fire, reward and penalize, so that employees will work for the organization's objectives.

The impact of this design-feature on human personality is clearly to make the individuals dependent on, passive and subordinate to the leader. The results are obviously to lessen their self-control and shorten their time-perspective. It would seem, then, that the design feature of hierarchic structure works against four of the growth lines, pushing individuals back from active toward passive, from equal toward subordinate, from self-controlled toward dependent, from being aware of long time-perspectives toward having only a short time-perspective. In all these four ways, the result is to move employees back from adulthood toward

Planners have tried to cushion this impact in several ways. First, they see to it that those who perform well in the hierarchy are rewarded. But the trouble with this is that the reward ought to be psychological as well as material—and yet, because of the job specialization which simplifies and does not satisfy a worker, few psychological rewards are possible. So the material reward has to seem more important, and has to be increased. To do this, however, means that one does nothing about the on-the-job situation that is causing the trouble, but instead pays the employee for the dissatisfaction he experiences. Obviously, management in doing this leaves an employee to feel that basic causes of dissatisfaction are built into industrial life, that the rewards received are wages for dissatisfaction, and that any satisfaction to be gained must be looked for outside the organization.

Other things are wrong with raising wages to make up for dissatisfaction. For it assumes that the worker can so split himself up that he can be quite satisfied with the anomalous situation we have just described him as being in. Second, it assumes he is mainly interested in what money can get. And third, it assumes he is best rewarded as an individual producer, without regard to the work group in which he belongs. This may well mean that a worker whose group informally sanctions holding production down will therefore have to choose between pleasing the boss and getting paid more, or pleasing his fellows and getting paid less.

A second solution has been suggested by planners: to have very good bosses. The leaders, that is, should be objective, rational and personify the reasonableness of the organizational structure. To do this means they keep from getting emotionally involved; as one executive states, "We must try to keep our personalities out of the job." Evaluating others, he sets aside his own feelings. And, of course, he must be loyal to the organization.

But this solution too violates some of the basic properties of personality. To split what one does from what one is, or to ask others to do it, is to violate one's self-integrity, and the same goes for the effort to keep personality out of the job. (As for impartiality, as May has pointed out, the best way to be impartial is to be as partial as one's needs require but stay aware of this partiality so as to correct for it at the moment of decision.)

One other solution has been offered: to encourage competition among employees, so as to get them to show initiative and creativity. Competing for promotions, this "rabble hypothesis" suggests, will increase the efficiency of the competitors.

Williams, however, conducting some controlled experiments, shows that this assumption is not necessarily valid for people placed in competitive situations. Deutsch supports Williams' results with extensive controlled research, and goes much further, suggesting that competitive situations make for so much tension that they lessen efficiency. Levy and Freedman confirm Deutsch's work and go on to relate competition to psychoneurosis.

We have looked at the design features of job specialization and hierarchic structure. A final principle of design is *unity of direction:* efficiency is supposed to increase if each administrative unit has a single activity planned and directed by a single leader. The implication is that this leader sets the goal, the conditions for meeting the goal, and the path toward it, for all his employees. If, because of job specialization, the workers are not personally interested in the work goal, then unity of direction creates the ideal conditions for psychological failure. For each individual basically (as we have said) aims at psychological success, which comes only when he defines his own goals, in relation to his personal needs and to the difficulties of reaching the goals.

What we have seen is that if we use the principles of

formal organization as ideally defined, employees will be working in an environment where (1) they have little or no control over their workaday world; (2) they are expected to be passive, dependent and subordinate; (3) they are expected to have a short time-perspective; (4) job specialization asks them to perfect and value only a few of their simplest abilities; and (5) they are asked to produce under conditions (imposed by the principle of unity of direction) ideal for psychological failure.

Since behavior in these ways is more childish than adult, it appears that formal organizations are willing to pay high wages and provide adequate seniority if mature adults will, for eight hours a day, behave like children. It is obvious that such behavior is incompatible with the human need to develop and "grow up." And it appears that the incongruency increases as (1) the employee is of greater maturity, (2) the formal structure is tightened in search of efficiency; (3) one goes down the line of command; (4) jobs become more mechanized.

That such incongruency will result in frustration, failure, short time-perspective and conflict hardly needs demonstration. How, in the face of all this, will the employee be able to maintain a sense of his own integrity? He will react in part like a turtle and in part like a porcupine: by leaving, by "ladder climbing" within the organization, by such defense reactions as daydreaming, aggression, ambivalence, regression, projection and so on; or by becoming apathetic toward the organization's makeup and goals. If this occurs, he will be apt to start "goldbricking" or even cheating. He may create informal groups who agree that it is right to be apathetic and uninvolved, and these informal groups may become formalized—instead of just gathering to gripe they will hold meetings and pass resolutions. Or he may take the view that money and "what's in it for me" have become the really important things about his work, and the psychological rewards are just malarkey. And he will end up by indoctrinating the new employees so that they will see the organization through the same mud-colored glasses as he does.

There is only one real way to improve the sad picture described above: by decreasing the dependency, decreasing the subordination, and decreasing the submissiveness expected of employees. It can be shown that making a job bigger—not more specialized and small—will help do these things; and that employee-centered (or democratic or participative) leadership also will improve the situation.

Yet, these remedies are limited, for they require employees who are already highly interested in the organization. And the situation which makes them needed is one in which employees are anything but interested. In such a situation, strongly directive leadership is almost necessary to get the apathetic employee to move at all. This in its own turn, helps to create the very problem it is trying to solve!

The dilemma, then, is basic and is a continuing challenge to the social scientist and the leader in an organization. They may well begin their efforts to work for a solution—one in which the organization will be as efficient as possible, while the people in it will be as free and strongly developing as possible—by considering two facts. The first is that no organization can be maximally efficient that stunts its own vital parts. And the second is that our culture and each of its institutions, from family through nations and beyond, are one vast interlocking set of organizations.

*July 1964*

# The Superior Person

ABRAHAM H. MASLOW

None of the writers that I have been reading on manage-ment dares to lock horns with the problem that is so unpopular in any democracy: that some people are superior to others in any specific skill, or—what is more provocative to the democrat—in *general* capacity. There is evidence that some people tend to be generally superior, that they are simply superior biological organisms born into the world.

The children studied by Lewis Terman in his *Genetic Studies of Genius* were originally included in the group solely on the basis of I.Q. scores; but they also proved to be healthier, stronger, bigger, more original, more creative, more energetic, more emotionally stable, more pesistent, with a broader range of interests and with a much higher level of academic accomplishment than control groups. Those signs of general superiority persisted beyond child-hood into maturity and were reflected in the very high-status jobs they came to hold. The follow-up for 35 years has shown that the superior child, with few exceptions, becomes the able adult, superior in nearly every aspect according to Terman.

Studies of the distribution of I.Q. scores show the rarity of the superior intelligence: scores of 120 to 140, regarded as evidence of a superior intellect, are achieved by only 11.3 percent of the population. Very superior intelligence, which can be defined as an I.Q. of over 140, occurs in only 1.15 percent of the population.

The implications of the existence of the generally superior person are fantastic and dangerous and perhaps more than a little frightening in a democracy. What this might imply for management and the work situation is also startling. If there are people who by heredity, constitution and biological endowment have an overall superiority, how does society deal with them? No society can function unless inferiors are able to admire superiors, or at least not to hate and attack them. No society can be really efficient unless its superior persons are preferred and elected by the other people.

This whole delicate problem is ducked by democrats. We don't talk about the people among us who are obviously inferior—the feeble-minded, the crippled, the senile —because this doesn't fit well with our political conceptions that call for one man, one vote. Democracy premises that men are equal. Yet there must be a good 10 percent of the population, at least, whom we simply tell what to do and whom we care for as if they were pet animals. Our society has never squarely faced the question of the objective superiority of some people and the inferiority of others. In fact, people who are superior at anything sometimes tend to feel guilty about it and to be apologetic. There are people who are "losers" in the sense that they can't bear to win; they get too disturbed and too guilty and they feel too selfish, too crass and too overbearing.

In our democratic society superiority is generally masked. Nobody runs around saying in company how superior he is; democrats are a tribe in which there are no chiefs, only Indians. But the fact remains that as psychological sciences move forward we do know more and more about ourselves. In a very objective way, I know what my I.Q. is and I know what my personality test scores are and what the Rorschach test shows, so that I can make a fairly factual summary of my abilities. It is permitted me to say in public what my weaknesses are, but it is certainly not permitted to me to say what my superiorities are. This is a real weakness in our society. We arrange things so that the boss or leader or general or successful person tends to be put on the defensive. Should this be so, in a perfectly mobile and ideal society in which cream does rise to the top? In an ideal society, prestige, power and ability would be perfectly correlated with actual capacity and skill and talent. We could define a good society as one in which all those who are on top deserve to be there.

The argument can be seen more clearly on the smaller canvas of the industrial organization. Here the values are simpler than in the political organization of society. In the ordinary industrial situation under competitive circumstances, simple pragmatic success and productivity mean industrial life or death. Factual superiority simply must be sought out there.

Traditional ideas of how to run an industrial enterprise rely almost solely on the use of pure power by the boss. He gives orders to subordinates who obey because they get paid to obey and/or because they will be fired if they don't obey.

The authoritarian type of management rests on certain assumptions about human behavior that social research has shown are erroneous. These assumptions, which have been called Theory X by McGregor, embody the traditional view of direction and control. The theory assumes that:

- the average human being dislikes work and will avoid it if he can;
- therefore, most people must be coerced, controlled, directed and threatened with punishment if they are to work adequately;
- the average human being prefers to be directed, wishes to avoid responsibility, has relatively little ambition and wants security above all things.

Modern theories of enlightened management insist that these classic, authoritarian ideas do not fit the situation, that they do not secure the highest levels of productivity and that they are undemocratic.

Enlightened management, as it is taught by the human relations practitioner, relies on a different set of assumptions. These assumptions, which here are called Theory Y, are in fact much closer to what social science research has shown are the truths of human behavior. Theory Y assumes:

- that work is a natural human activity;
- that men will work toward goals to which they are committed without coercion, and that commitment follows from the opportunity to realize their own potentialities;
- that most men have a higher level of intellectual capacity than the usual conditions of modern industrial life reveal.

Proper management techniques provide employees with opportunities to develop their abilities by participation; in developing themselves they become involved in and committed to the organization. Embodying the traditional view of direct participation, McGregor, one of the leading exponents of human relations ideology puts it: "Theory Y ... places problems squarely in the lap of management. If employees are lazy, indifferent, unwilling to take responsibility, intransigent, uncreative, uncooperative, Theory Y implies that the causes lie in management's methods of organization and control."

The best thing about this new outlook on management is that from whichever point you start, whether from the point of view of what is best for making a profit or from the point of view of what is best for the personal development of the employees, the result is the same. That which is good for personal development is also good for turning out good automobiles and for having a well-run organization that will last for a long time.

First of all, let's state clearly that the kind of industrial setup that sends its executives to human relations training sessions is a special and highly selected environment. The unselected differentiated population at large has a fair proportion of very sick people, very incompetent people, very psychopathic people, insane people, vicious people, authoritarian people, immature people. Any reasonably intelligent personnel policy will exclude many of these diminished and inadequate people that one finds in any larger society. Even within this selected environment, the human relations techniques under discussion here refer exclusively to executive personnel; for example, top management vis-a-vis middle management. Writings in this field tend to imply a much broader applicability.

The writers on the new style of management have a tendency to indulge in certain pieties and dogmas of democratic management that are sometimes in striking contrast to the realities of the situation. Robert Tannenbaum in *Leadership and Organization* says, for instance, "Managers differ greatly in the amount of trust they have in other people," as if trust depended entirely on the character of the manager. Surely trustfulness depends also on who the manager is dealing with. To trust psychopaths or paranoiacs is not generous but foolish. Any outlook which encourages us to trust everybody is an unrealistic dogma.

In a paper delivered at an International Management Congress in 1963, Rensis Likert described some central concepts of enlightened management, including the following:

> Each member of the organization ... should have adequate levels of interaction skills to perform well the functions of the position he occupies. The interaction skills include skills in the leadership and membership roles, in effective group functioning including problem solving, and skill in maintaining an understanding and supportive relationship with the other members of one's work group. *In addition, each member of the organization should have sufficient amounts of both technical and administrative skills to carry out well the duties of his position.*

The italics are mine, but the placement at the end of the paragraph and the afterthought nature of the phrasing are Likert's. Again the dogma of human relations comes first; the objective requirements of the situation are secondary.

With dogma occupying this front-rank position, it is not surprising that human relations theory has evaded the problem of the very superior boss. The participative kind of management, where subordinates work together toward a good solution to a problem, is often an inappropriate setting for the superior boss. He is apt to get restless and irritated; keeping his mouth shut can be physical torture. The less intelligent subordinates are also affected adversely. Why should they sweat for three days to work toward the solution of a particular problem when they know all the time that the superior can see the solution in three minutes. Their tendency is to become passive and resentful of the boss's superiority. Group dynamics approaches here are phony and can only breed resentment.

The best way to handle the problem of the very superior boss might be to try to analyze what makes a boss superior and how he functions best, without any obeisance at all to democratic dogma. A functional boss is a person whose qualities suit him for being a leader. In accordance with the objective demands of reality, the leader ought to be more efficient, more capable, more talented than the follower. The optimum arrangement of an industrial organization would be one that provided this functional boss with an environment best suited to the advancement of the organization's aims. This situation should be, that is, synergic. Synergy, as I use the term (following Ruth Benedict), refers to a situation so arranged that each person involved, by pursuing his own selfish aims, aids the other people involved and the institution itself. For an industrial situation to be synergic, the special qualities of the superior boss must be actually encouraged. A functionally good boss is, among other things, someone who needs to have his own way and gets special pleasure from it. A man who is a functionally good boss is someone who gets a special kick out of doing a good job, or seeing a good job done, or forming an efficient smooth-running organization, or turning out an especially good product. It is a kind of high-level instinct of workmanship.

If the industrial situation is properly set up, this hypothetical boss, by doing just what pleases him most and by getting rid of what irritates him most, is doing exactly what is best for the institution.

The highly directive leader (not the only effective kind) probably has a strong sense of order and completeness— he's the kind of person who simply has to straighten that crooked picture on the wall. This is the person who *needs* to perfect the environment; having the power to do this seems a wonderful thing to him. In the early days of World War II, when Churchill, as First Lord of the Admiralty, had only limited control over British Military policy, he was ridden by the deepest anxiety. When, at a very dark moment in Britain's history, he became prime minister, he wrote, "I was conscious of a profound sense of relief. At last I had the authority to give directions over the whole scene . . . I slept soundly and had no need for cheering dreams. Facts are better than dreams."

The dominant leader may differ from the more passive person in his physiological makeup. There is a body of experimental data from animals which would confirm such an idea. It may be that people are actually born different with respect to need to control, need to defer, need to be passive or to be active, etc. Those managers who do function best as highly directive leaders (probably as a result of the constitutional endowments we have been discussing) must not be dogmatically rejected as anti-democratic. Some situations demand the highly directive leader—to captain a ship or to command an army group; other situations realistically demand the team sharer. We have to accept both kinds of leaders, and try to fit the right manager to the right situation.

The relationship of the boss to the people whom he might have to order around or fire or punish is, if we are realistic about it, not a friendly relation among equals. Our attitude toward anyone who has power over us, even if it is the most benevolent power, is different from our attitude toward those who are equals. This hard reality ought to have some impact on the theories of participative, democratic management. In many situations, if the boss is going to be able to exercise the unpleasant, dominating boss functions when they should be exercised, it may be best to maintain a certain distance, objectivity and detachment from those whom he might have to discipline.

Because the boss is really *not* one of the boys, he cannot be as expressive and open about his own thoughts and anxieties as the others are permitted and encouraged to be. A successful boss must have the power and the ability to keep his mouth shut, not to depress or upset the morale of his workers. He must be able to take upon his own shoulders the worry and anxiety and tensions that may arise from a particular situation.

There is also the question of whether the democratic, participative style of leadership always best serves the needs of the followers. This is doubtful. It depends on the nature of the situation and of the abilities of the subordinates. For dependent, poorly educated types, decisiveness can be very attractive. This can explain the attraction of paranoid leaders like Hitler or Stalin or McCarthy; the decisiveness of the paranoid authoritarian relieves the followers of all anxiety. The decisiveness, without the paranoia, remains a characteristic of the functional boss.

In short, the good boss is psychologically healthy. He is healthy enough to make and impose unpopular decisions if that is what the situation demands. He is healthy enough to relinquish control if his primary aim is to develop the capacities of his subordinates and if the situation permits such an approach.

I think the way I would sum up some of my uneasiness about the management and leadership literature and my fear of a new kind of piety and dogma would be to shift the center of attention from the person of the leader to the objective requirements of the particular situation or problem. The stress should be on facts, knowledge, and skill rather than on communication, democracy, human relations and good feeling. There ought to be a bowing to the authority of the facts.

This shift in emphasis is not a rejection of what human relations theory has to say about management. The facts *do* tend to support participative management insofar as the culture is good enough, the people involved are psychologically healthy, and the general conditions are good. More stress needs to be placed on the leader's ability to perceive the truth, to be correct, to be tough and stubborn and decisive in terms of the facts. There ought to be more stress on knowledge and experience—on real, objective superiority —than there is now. In an ideal society it seems very clear that people must be able to admire, to choose and to follow the superior leader with a minimum of antagonism toward his superiority. I am stressing this because I am so aware of the fact that real factual superiors tend to be strongly resented as well as admired, and that therefore they are less apt to be chosen on the basis of a democratic vote.

We must work out some better criterion for selecting leaders than popularity. It may be that if we shift attention to what the facts demand, to factual superiority, to the authority of the truth, that we are then somewhat more apt to get the best leader, from the pragmatic point of view. We must learn to choose superior people and to value them even if we don't love them, or if they make us uncomfortable, or if they throw us into conflict, or if they make us doubt our own worth a little bit. The good society is impossible unless we develop the ability to admire superiority.

*May 1964*

# The Trouble
# with Democratic Management

### WILLIAM GOMBERG

When Florence Nightingale was fighting to impose the rigid standards of sanitation on male nurses who were resisting her "new fangled feminine" ideas during the Crimean War, she was fond of repeating her favorite maxim: "Whatever else a hospital should be, it should not be a source of infection."

An adaptation of her phrase to university life seems nowhere more appropriate than in the prestigious business schools of the great universities. Whatever else a university should be, it should not be a source of confusion.

But many university business schools are sources of serious confusion in their dissemination of the most fashionable current cliche in discussions about the changing nature of management—*that it must become democratic or perish.* Democratic management of industry has become the most modish philosophy shared by the *avant garde* students of the American industrial enterprise. Its votaries are found not only among the leading academic figures in our prestigious business schools, but also include the public relations counselors of some of our leading industrial organizations.

"Democracy" is among the most misused words in our vocabulary. Just as the loose use of "love" encompasses diversity ranging from an obsessive need for possession accompanied by hate to intense joy joined by mutual growth, so democracy is used as a catchall for management philosophies ranging from participative play acting under the benevolent aegis of an autocrat to just plain autocratic decentralization.

It is well that we take a realistic look at what democracy means in our polity before we recommend it for business application irrespective of the economic technologies and marketing constraints governing the enterprise.

Democracy is essentially a means of distributing power in society so that no single institution—political, social, or economic—is able to dominate the complete society. More often than not, these institutions, whether trade unions, business enterprises, or professional organizations, constitute oligarchies that receive and are only entitled to receive a partial commitment of their constituents' loyalty and interests.

Those same people are committed to different organizations at different times depending upon which of their needs is being served. The same person is associated as an employee with a business enterprise, as a voter with a political party, as a professional with a professional society, etc. Democracy is served when all of these institutions strive to outdo each other in relative achievements, in an instutionalized climate, so that no single institution receives, or is entitled to receive, a full and absolute personal committment from anybody.

Much of the campaign for "democracy" in industry is prompted by efforts to secure a fuller personal commitment for the enterprise from its working constituents than may be warranted by a rational program for a "full life."

This campaign does not flow from any conscious conspiracy of an exploiting class to do in an exploited class, but from a mistaken view of both the purpose and needs of the enterprise.

Warren Bennis of the Massachusetts Institute of Technology has enunciated a set of values for the new kinds of knowledge-oriented corporations which he associates with democracy. It is his position that these new organizations must make use of democracy as an administrative technique because they are based upon scientific effort. Scientific effort in turn, he asserts, can only flourish in the open society.

Before we even list this system of values, it would be well to remind ourselves that both Nazi Germany and the Soviet Union, hardly notable examples of the open society, were and are flourishing technologically. Had the Nazis allocated their scientific resources to atomic energy instead of to rocketry, the entire story of the war might have been different. Some military observers have speculated that had the war lasted a few more months, the German superiority in rocketry may have easily generated a stalemate.

The value structure which Philip Slater and Bennis propose *(Harvard Business Review,* March 1964) for industrial management follows:

■ Full and free *communication,* regardless of rank and power;

■ A reliance on *consensus,* rather than the more customary forms of *coercion* or compromise to manage conflict;

■ The idea that *influence* is based on technical competence and knowledge rather than on the vagaries of personal whims or prerogatives of power;

■ An atmosphere that permits and even encourages emotional *expression* as well as task oriented acts;

■ A basically *human* bias, one that accepts the inevitability of conflict between the organization and the individual, but which is willing to cope with and mediate this conflict on rational grounds.

This value structure is definitely on the side of the angels. The real problem, however, is to what extent is it a realistic assessment of the managerial task? Many of these values have been accepted as early as the beginning of the study of management. Some of them are singularly inappropriate.

If we return to the writings of Frederick W. Taylor, generally acknowledged as the founder of the scientific management school (or cult, depending upon your prejudices) we find that his concept of functional foremanship is based completely upon the idea that influence should be based upon technical competence and knowledge. In fact he was the embodiment of the typical modern authoritarian intellectual who is all for consensus provided it is based upon his own concept of rationality. Taylor would not have a man give orders to another unless the order-giver enjoyed superior knowledge over the order-taker. His approach was completely pragmatic. "Status must be based upon superior knowledge rather than nepotism or superior financial power." The weakness in Taylor's scheme was his inability to understand the power paradox that expresses itself in the title of a popular song of a bygone day, "Who Takes Care of the Caretaker's Daughter, when the Caretaker Is Busy Taking Care?" Taylor's industrial organization suffered from the same deficiencies that plagued Plato's philosopher state. Who chooses the philosophers and the philosophers' successors?

Taylor failed to understand how to check superior power when it arrogated to itself the arbitrary judgment of what was superior knowledge. Bennis is no more successful than Taylor in resolving this dilemma. Both depend upon the good will and good sense of the power wielder to show self restraint. Both are describing benevolent autocracy. This is hardly meant to be critical. There is great doubt that these autonomous institutions can be run effectively except as benevolent autocracies. Democracy is served by the external checks on the autocrat outside of his institutional boundary. The competition of other industrial organizations is a check on the irrational confusion between superior status and superior knowledge.

Let us take an illustration of the way this democracy works industrially. The attack at Pearl Harbor cut us off from our Indonesian rubber supply. The state of chemical research divided experts into two camps—the advocates of an immediate investment in synthetic rubber plants based upon a petro-chemical process on the one hand and those who advocated plants based upon a grain alcohol process on the other.

Full and free communication among scientists had prevailed. There was no lack of emotional commitment in advocacy. The conflict between individual human aspirations and organizational constraints were only too clear to all. Quite obviously a consensus was impossible and time was of the essence. The solution—a bureaucratically imposed decision to follow one of the two lines of endeavor (the petro-chemical process) after listening to emotionally charged arguments on each side.

The same problem of consensus plagues a state highway commission when it seeks to clear an expressway route through a highly populated area. Every vested interest introduces its scientific experts, both social and engineering, to advocate alternatives for different "scientific" reasons, each of which contradicts the other. Ultimately, a bureaucrat imposes a decision.

In other words, managerial behavior was dictated by the nature of the technology and the economic constraints of limited available resources. Someone had to assume responsibility for the ultimate decision, and others were bound to be frustrated by the decision.

When American industry had grown so large that it had become necessary to decentralize marketing and production functions, this move was followed by much nonsensical talk about the democratization of industry. Decentralization was an attempt to maintain central control by sloughing off the less critical functions from the center. The choice was not between central control and control at the grass roots, but between carefully structured decentralization or unstructured decentralization on the basis of "squatters' rights."

For example: Before the duPonts took over control of the General Motors Corporation from Durant, the organization was a loose federation of companies organized along brand lines, each of which was free to make its own major capital expenditure decisions free of any control. Inasmuch as Durant did not provide for structured decentralization, the heads of the subsidiary companies moved into the vacuum and exercised the financial function by default. The result was that the organization was brought to the verge of bankruptcy until rescued by the duPonts who put Alfred Sloan in command. Sloan immediately centralized the financial function leaving other activities decentralized.

What is generally overlooked in studies of decentralization is that no successful firm ever decentralized the financial function. There was never more than one treasurer to a firm and the centralized control of finances exercised the ultimate power over all members of the decentralized facility. Here again a technique of centralized control was confused with democracy. The computer which multiplies the control area of the central office is leading to recentralization of control without any nonsense about participative decision-making at the grass roots.

Other observers, like Chris Argyris of Yale, link democratization of industry with movements like the sensitivity training programs associated with the National Training Laboratories. Others have associated democratization programs with group dynamics based upon the philosophy of the late Kurt Lewin, a well-known social psychologist.

There are two shortcomings to most of these proposed solutions:

■ The first is the avoidance of coming to grips with the fundamental problems posed by the locus of power in our industrial structure.

■ The second lies in the implicit morality attending the use of quasi-psychotherapeutic techniques for industrial purposes.

William F. Whyte, a prominent social anthropologist has called the attention of his colleagues to the dangers of the techniques which they are employing. He warns, ". . . many of the problems that management people get into in trying to use human relations knowledge arise through a failure to recognize the power factor. There tends to be an assumption that if you just learn the techniques, you can ignore power, or better yet, you can establish a greater power differential between yourself in management and your subordinates."

A good example of this kind of manipulation comes from a widely hailed experiment in which behavioral scientists were under the impression that they were proving the effectiveness of democratic participative management when they were actually engaging in involuntary manipulation.

I am referring to the Harwood experiment which has been referred to in the literature *ad nauseam* as an example of the results that can be expected from participative management. Paradoxically it demonstrates what can be expected from manipulative management.

The Harwood Pajama Factory located in Marion, Virginia, was described as industrial "heaven" by a *Fortune* writer, "where unions seem unable to make headway." The writer noted that at Marion "team captains" elected by the workers and foremen engaged in free discussion. They considered the level of production and the company's hopes for raising it. They "voluntarily" then set a standard in excess of what management would have established unilaterally.

The *Fortune* article came to the attention of the International Ladies' Garment Workers' Union which dispatched an organizer to the factory.

The town of Marion, in the heart of Senator Byrd's political area, hardly offers a salubrious climate for organization. Yet the factory—"where unions seem unable to make headway"—was organized in a record short time. The details of the experiments which were going on reveal that what the management called "worker participation" was experienced by the group as *manipulation*. This explained the readiness with which the group embraced the union.

The general intent of these experiments was to demonstrate how participation by members of the group in a group decision could be used to overcome resistance to change and increase production. The experimenter discovered what Stanley Mathewson had observed as early as 1931 that unorganized workers protect themselves against the threatened "speedups" by the organization of secret groups.

They classified these groups as follows:

■ strong psychological subgroups with high "we-feeling" and *negative* attitudes towards management;

■ strong psychological groups with high "we-feeling" and *positive* attitudes towards management.

The former work against management to restrict production. The latter work with management to increase production.

The remedy: an opportunity for participation by the members of the negative group in a decision to increase production. Equivalent groups of similar productivity and "we feeling" characteristics were selected and each was treated in one of three ways:

■ GROUP 1. Meetings were held with the management and "representatives" of the group to fix the new working procedures and the production norms to go with the working procedure.

■ GROUP 2. Meetings were held in the same fashion with all the members of the group instead of representatives.

■ GROUP 3. The control group was left to the classical routine of an assignment without the benefit of ceremony.

The results were as follows:

■ GROUP 2. The full participant group showed the most satisfactory improvement in performance.

■ GROUP 1. The representative group showed an improvement, but not quite as high as the full participant group.

■ GROUP 3. The control group showed conventional improved performance.

Conclusion of the experimenter: Full "democratic participation by the workers in decision making is a valuable managerial instrument to improve production."

There are some questions that might be put by any thoughtful observer:

Is this democratic participation in management or is it a cleverly contrived managerial device to break up the solidarity of the group? How free would workers feel to decline the management invitation to increase production —when they enjoyed none of the protections of industrial due process? How much real participation was there in defining mutual objectives, or did management define the objective and then "democratically" manipulate the workers as means? Would the workers have responded as readily to encouragement to increase production unless they felt threatened by this kind of manipulative democracy in which they were invited to undress publicly?

The psychologist seemed completely unaware of the power structure of a modern factory in which the consultees enjoy none of the protections of due process.

When the union officers, in the early stages of unionization, made the mistake of behaving like statesmen toward this kind of manipulation (which they did not understand completely), the factory elected an aggressive shop steward who damned both the union's officers and the plant management. Dr. Marrow, the company president, came down to visit the plant with a staff member of the union's engineering department and departed hastily when he saw the violence of the workers' feelings.

This Harwood experiment and its outcome are particularly interesting because they represent a bridgehead between the old clinical "human relations" movement and the more modern "behavioral science" enthusiasm. The management enthusiasm for the human relations movement is more likely to be explained by the date of publication of its classical presentation in 1938, rather than by any of the concrete formulae it offered for management voluntary indoctrination or involuntary manipulation of their subordinates. It will be recalled that the Wagner Labor Act was validated unexpectedly by the Supreme Court in 1937. Management was caught completely unprepared to deal with trade unions and here was a voice out of the wilderness offering management both an explanation and a remedy for the predicament in which it found itself.

It is important to keep in mind that much of the material celebrating participative management or so-called democracy in industry flowed largely from an unspoken conviction—unless both the porter and the president look upon their work place as the site not only of their working interests but the very core of their *whole human interest,* then there was an important social problem seeking solution.

It is understandable why work would be the core of interest for the president of a corporation. From the focus of a porter, however, this proposition becomes somewhat more difficult to accept no matter how democratic you make house cleaning.

I have heard Franklin Folts of Harvard describe the typical member of the Harvard Business School's middle management program—someone completely involved in his work, dedicated to the firm's business interests on a full-time basis, self-confident of his ability to solve all business problems, though somewhat fearful and resentful of union "irrationality." Professor Folts expressed dismay that so many of these men, whose average age is thirty-two, were so completely involved in their work, eschewing any diversion, that they were showing symptoms like peptic ulcers and high blood pressure.

Now management programs at universities (at Harvard and elsewhere) hope not only to equip men with problem solving skills, but to contribute to the full development of their complete human potential. However, if the professors who are dedicated to this proposition really mean what they say about full human development, then a company executive might think twice before sending any of his young men to their institutions, lest he return home vocationally disabled.

Let us assume that the executive in question is the president of the XYZ Automobile Corporation and employs a sales manager, utterly dedicated to the proposition that life's most important task is placing two XYZ automobiles in every citizen's garage. This is the sales manager's twenty-four hour objective and he is doing it successfully. His personality profile is exactly that described by Franklin Folts. He now arrives at the university and it proceeds to expand his horizons. He learns that there are active interests, music, art, and opera to compete for those twenty-four hours, previously devoted to pushing automobile sales.

A psychiatrist might hail the "new man" as a success. After all, is there any doubt that Professor Folts was describing the classic profile of a compulsive, obsessive neurotic? Now the sales manager is no longer a neurotic, he is a full human being, he has even developed his doubts that the most important aim in life is putting two brand new XYZ automobiles in every citizen's garage. The question remains, is this full human being merely a euphemism for a disabled sales manager?

Between 1946 and 1956, American business did not have to face this question squarely. It is the writer's conviction that this decade will go down in history as the "golden age of the staff." The reason for this golden age is not too difficult to find. Any enterprise of any size could not help making money during this decade. The country was on a consumer goods binge in the wake of World War II and the Korean conflict.

Enterprises like the Studebaker corporation displayed much more interest in vague industrial citizenship responsibilities than they did in meeting competition. The discipline exerted by the economic law of "avoiding a loss" was lax indeed. Human relationists and behavioral scientists had a ball glorifying companies whose executives were more worried about their personal image than their economic performance. But it would be a foolish worker indeed, or for that matter, a foolish middle-management executive, who given a long-run choice between Studebaker democracy and General Motors authoritarianism over the long run, would prefer Studebaker's South Bend funeral in 1964 to the full employment opportunities currently offered by General Motors. The General Motors authoritarianism is constrained by an aggressive independent union, but it is master in its own house within these constraints.

Naturally a democratic society does not leave autonomous business institutions free to impose their economic objectives upon the public without any countervailing constraints, but it is important to remember that our corporate heads are assigned the task of economic performance, not emotional rehabilitation. They are not heads of state and must behave rationally and economically within the set of constraints imposed by the other values of the over-all society, but the chief criterion against which they will be judged must remain economic performance.

Benevolent autocrats operating within a competitive institutional framework seem to provide the most effective

combination of economic achievement and political re-
straints. Industry's democrats have confused a benevolent
paternal style of velvet-gloved autocracy with democracy.
The style of permissive management should not be confused with the essence of democracy, the distribution of
real power.

Professor William M. Evans of MIT has raised the
real question about democracy in the modern corporation:
how much protection of due process is enjoyed by *the
ranks of middle management* in its relationships with top
management? Play-acting in benevolent autocracies is no
more the answer to this problem than company unions
were the answer for the work force.

*July/August 1966*

# Gray Flannel Unionist

ADOLF STURMTHAL

We are beginning to witness a trend toward the development of two different kinds of unionism in the western world. I suggest that we tentatively call them bargaining unions and administrative unions. Whether a union falls into one category or the other depends upon the role it chooses to play in the context of industrial democracy.

■ For bargaining unions, industrial democracy is limited to bargainable issues and the proper locale of industrial democracy is the plant where union action is direct and close to the rank and file.

■ For administrative unions, it means impact on top policy-making bodies; these unions find their leverage strongest above the plant level. They are willing to accept some degree of managerial responsibility; they deal with employers' associations on an industry-wide basis (thus securing for themselves a voice in the distribution of the increment in national income as it grows from year to year) ; and they participate in the work of government planning agencies.

Industrial democracy is a vague term, one that can be shaped according to the needs of the moment. To some observers it means simply a collective bargaining relationship in which the workers or their representatives share with management in the determination of their wages and working conditions. Other writers use the term to refer to a general cooperation between labor and management on all matters of common interest. In a third and most significant usage, industrial democracy denotes a social and economic system in which labor completely assumes the function of management.

The idea of industrial democracy can be traced back to the latter half of the 19th century. It has its roots in the Syndicalist movement as it was worked out in France and spread to Spain and Italy, and in the Guild Socialist movement in England. Guild Socialism and French Syndicalism both had an impact on the Industrial Workers of the World (the Wobblies) in the United States. But the most significant event in the evolution of the concept was probably the Russian revolution. In the immediate aftermath of revolution the Bolsheviks—knowing that the existing managerial class was hostile to their regime and believing that management did not require any special skills in any case —handed over the administration of industry to representatives of the workers. (The management of industry by workers in the USSR ended with the introduction of the New Economic Policy in 1921, and the practice was not resumed even when the NEP was superseded by the first five-year plan and the move toward an entirely state-run economy.)

After World War I the idea of industrial democracy revived in the West in the form of a merger between the ideas of Guild Socialism and those of the Russian Revolution. Socialist parties in Austria and Germany advocated a system of nationalized industry which would be administered by representatives of government, consumers, and labor. French trade unions adopted the same program. In England, Guild Socialism reached its height by 1920 and then declined rapidly in influence. When the idea of nationalization came up again with the increase in Labor Party strength in the late 1930s, very little was left of the Guild Socialist influence. The nationalization laws enacted when the Labor Party came to power in 1945 provided for management by experts (including experts in personnel management and industrial relations) but not for representation of employees or their unions. Only some vague and unconvincing clauses about consultation remained in the nationalization laws as a last vestige of the ideas of Guild Socialism.

On the continent, the end of World War II brought a temporary revival of industrial democracy; workers' councils were reconstituted in the factories; in Germany a codetermination system in coal and steel and the Works' Constitutional Law were established; in France personnel delegates, plant committees, and institutions for worker participation in the management of nationalized enterprises were set up; the *Commissione Interne* (a form of workers' council), were established in Italy. After this first spate of post war activity, interest in industrial democracy in Western Europe lapsed once more.

Despite these periodic eclipses, the term "industrial democracy" has come back into use again and again. Undoubtedly one of the reasons for the longevity of the term is its vagueness. It can be used to cover a broad range of worker participation in industry. At the same time, the ambiguity of the term has made it difficult to evaluate the effectiveness of any particular system of industrial democracy. We lack a yardstick by which to measure the distance between goal and attainment. For a fruitful discussion of the various ideas, plans, and institutions that come under the heading of industrial democracy, we must set up some kind of analytical scheme. We can base such a scheme on the proposition that all the ideas about industrial democracy, and all the institutions that result from those ideas, have this common ground: they are all intended to give workers or their representatives an influence on some aspects of the workers' life in the plant.

Starting from that proposition, we can distinguish among the various schemes according to:

■ the degree of influence which workers attain. Here we separate simple consultation from co-decision making (the power to veto), with a number of possible variants.

■ the subjects on which workers have influence. The "subject matter" of influence can range from the traditional topics of collective bargaining such as wages and working conditions to technical, commercial, and financial problems.

■ whether the influence is exerted directly or through representatives. Influence might be exerted directly by "workers' collectives" as they are called in Eastern Europe, or by delegates in workers' councils, or by representatives in managerial and administrative bodies. In general, the higher the level at which influence is exerted, the greater the probability that influence is exerted through representatives or delegates.

■ the level of management or of public administration at which worker influence is brought to bear. This level may be a single plant, an entire industry, the whole industrial complex of a nation, or the highest levels of economic administration in the government itself.

I should like to use this framework to consider the current labor movement in the industrial nations of the West, with a brief reference to the countries belonging to the Eastern bloc as well.

A number of institutions, of various types, were established in Western Europe after the war which were designed as instruments of workers' participation in management. These institutions sought to provide for labor influence at various levels of the economic hierarchy, from the plant or individual firm all the way up to the top policy-making bodies in the country. In the terms of our analytical scheme, the following observations about the goals and the performance of these institutions are important:

■ The power of institutions at the plant level was greatest in the area of wages and working conditions. Councils and other institutions of industrial democracy frequently had a veto power on issues relating to hiring and firing, particularly of large groups.

■ In the areas of technical, financial, and commercial interests the influence of low-level groups was usually limited to consultation.

■ Workers showed least concern in the areas of finance, economics, and technicology.

■ Consultation at high governmental levels is more and more the accepted practice in Western nations, regardless of the political color of the government.

■ Participation involving some degree of managerial responsibility, such as union representation in the administration of nationalized enterprises in France, is still limited to only a part of the Western world.

In general, the institutions of industrial democracy seem to have performed best with regard to the traditional subject matter of collective bargaining. There are a number of reasons, from both the labor and the management perspective, why this should have been so.

On the union side there was, in some countries, reluctance to commit labor to managerial responsibility. Official British Trades Union Congress policy was and continues to be based on the proposition that "the union cannot sit on both sides of the bargaining table." British (and American) unions regard collective bargaining and grievance handling as their primary function; if they accepted managerial responsibility they would no longer be free to pursue this basic duty. (German and French unions seem to have made the opposite choice. They have left the bulk of grievance handling to the workers' councils—essentially non-union organizations—and devote a large and increasing portion of their energy to influencing general economic policy at management and governmental levels.)

Management, whenever possible, tended to narrow council activities by giving the workers' representatives real power of decision or co-decision only on issues of welfare and industrial relations. Management was least willing to encourage the councils in economic and technical matters, which they regarded as the almost exclusive preserve of managerial prerogative. On matters of this nature, management was rarely willing to go beyond superficial suggestion and consultation schemes.

The official reasons given by management for its reluctance to allow worker participation in these areas are:

■ employees are not competent to discuss economic and technical matters;

■ employees are not interested in these matters; and

■ even if employees were competent and interested, their influence would have an unfavorable effect on efficiency.

This concern with efficiency dominates most discussions of industrial democracy. The underlying assumption is either that the shortsightedness of employees will cause them to favor measures likely to impair efficiency, or that there is a basic conflict between the interests of employees and those of stockholders. (This latter point of view involves an amazing degree of acceptance of the Marxian world view by the managerial classes.) Concern with efficiency, oddly enough, appears to be most intense in countries with high or even highest output per man hour, where the sacrifice of some part of this efficiency in favor of other values (such as the expression of the human personality in the work process) could be most easily tolerated. Of course, this may be a chicken-egg problem. It could very well be that these countries are so efficient because they have been willing to subordinate other values to that of producing the highest possible output per man hour. And indeed the very existence of "moonlighting" may indicate that the dedication to maximum incomes is not necessarily limited to management. In any case, whether we approve or disapprove on moral or cultural grounds, efficiency is primary in Western industrial societies; for now at least, it is an unchangeable premise of social action in this field.

But even if we accept the idea that we in the West have an over-riding commitment to efficiency there is no convincing evidence that industrial democracy is detrimental to efficiency. Granted that, in the short run, employees or their representatives might tend to curtail investment funds in favor of current consumption (which may or may not be economically justified at any given time) or resist technological change; still the impact of industrial democracy may be quite different over the long run and in periods of full employment. Experience may change the character of workers' participation in management, may teach a better understanding of the connection between loss of current income and increased future earnings, and may open up new sources of technological and other improvements.

Moreover, there is no reason to assume that our society has fully solved the problem of identifying managerial talent or of providing the necessary channels of promotion. The ranks of the workers may prove to be a reservoir of managerial talent. What is more, the general level of employee competence is not fixed, but tends to rise as educational levels rise in the entire population. A growing proportion of the industrial labor force consists of white-collar workers and professional personnel and is eminently qualified to understand the economic, technical, and financial problems of management. Where workers have displayed little interest in these areas, the existing institutions of industrial democracy have often been limited to consultation; in the absence of real authority, workers are inclined to feel frustrated, to regard consultation as not much more than prior notification of management's intention.

Perhaps the most significant observation about the postwar Western European experiments in industrial democracy concerns their timing. The flurry of legislation creating these institutions after World War II was followed by an almost complete pause in experimentation. The German Works' Constitution Law set the final point, at least for an entire decade or more, to the series of acts unleashed by the shift in the relationship of social forces following the war and the defeat of Hitlerism. Since then, no further steps have been taken in the West to advance the cause of industrial democracy—apart from some small scale, minor experiments and De Gaulle's not very successful attempt to develop profit sharing. Indeed, the evolution of the existing institutions has tended to weaken industrial self-government in practice. The Italian *Commissione Interne* and the French plant committees have been gradually reduced to grievance-handling and the administration of welfare agencies in the plant. Their impact upon the technical, commercial, and financial operations of the enterprise is, in most cases, negligible. The affluent society of the West rejects daring experiments in plant management. The solution to the problem of worker alienation is no longer sought through reform of the enterprise, but more and more by offering compensation in the form of higher living standards and shorter work hours. The worker is less and less expected to find self-fulfillment in his work; his real life begins after working hours.

In the newly industrializing countries, the prospects of industrial democracy seem brighter. The need to locate scarce managerial talent, to accommodate the politically influential union movement, and to find new social and economic structures to replace those discredited by revolution have led to considerable experimentation in management. These experiments have involved participation at different levels—from the business firm up to government administration. This trend has been accentuated by the strength of anti-capitalistic sentiments in many countries. Workers' councils appear as desirable substitutes for private, owner-appointed managements.

In some of the countries of the Soviet bloc this pattern of industrial democracy has been re-emerging—with considerable ups and downs—since 1956. Leadership in these experiments has been held by the Yugoslav Workers' Council, a highly limited attempt to combine two types of industrial democracy: the workers' collective to represent industrial democracy in the plant, and the union to operate at the higher administrative levels. But even if the Councils were to perform effectively as managerial agencies—a large question by itself—the absence of democratic institutions at the higher policy-making levels would defeat any intention of turning unions into real agencies of industrial democracy. Moreover, the absence of aggressive workers' representation in the plant makes the system heavily weighted in favor of administrative objectives. This weighting is, of course, in line with the stated purpose of the governing party to achieve the highest possible rate of industrialization. Thus there is a built-in conflict between the objective of hothouse industrialization and both industrial self-government in the plant and normal union functions at higher administrative levels.

In a somewhat similar fashion, Western unions are confronted with a dilemma. The alternatives faced by Western labor movements can be described in a simplified way as power at the top or power at the bottom of the industrial relations system. It does not seem to be possible to exert these two kinds of power simultaneously; indeed it seems that the two are inversely related to each other. Involvement in management most often weakens the impact of the union at the bargaining table. The greater the degree of managerial responsibility one accepts, the less one is able to exert force from the outside. Yet primary absorption in the strategy of bargaining requires a refusal to use the means of influencing decisions which might be put at labor's disposal by the acceptance of managerial responsibility. Rank and file union members find it difficult to adjust to union participation in management. At one French union congress, for instance, one of the delegates complained about the ambiguous position of the union representatives in the managing board of the nationalized coal mines. "When I encounter them," the delegate said, "I do not know whether I am speaking to Comrade X or my boss."

American unions have generally avoided the dangers which such ambiguity could create. Yet they have not been altogether successful in this effort. Thus the growing influence of the unions in the White House and on Capitol Hill has both advantages and disadvantages. A powerful union can expect that its president will be consulted by the President of the United States and by Congress in the formation of economic policy. Governmental influence has been exerted in the union's behalf, by White House intervention in contract negotiations, by favorable legislation, and in many other ways. In exchange, the union not only tries to influence the votes of its members, but sometimes also adapts its strategy to the political needs of the incumbent in the White House. The price of the union's political influence is a restriction of its freedom at the bargaining table.

Similarly, ex-President David McDonald's friendship with leaders of industry may serve the union well in its efforts on behalf of its members. At the same time, the feeling that the union leader had become estranged from the rank and file by the closeness of his associations with management contributed to his recent defeat by I. W. Abel in their contest for the union presidency.

This, of course, is a long way off the Continental European system of union involvement in managerial responsibility. But in the countries of Western Europe (and to a lesser extent in the United States as well), there is a trend toward the adoption of democratic mechanisms of economic planning. If labor's views are to be considered in such a planning process, then unions will have to reconsider their attitudes toward involvement in managerial problems. In increasingly planned economies, the question facing unions becomes not whether they should participate in management, but how.

*July/August 1965*

# How Much Money Do Executives Want

### EDWARD E. LAWLER III

What are the most important rewards in an executive's life? To many businessmen the answer is simple and obvious: money. The expression "private enterprise," repeated so frequently and fondly, often means simply the chance to make money.

But behavioral science research and thought over the past several decades have put a host of modifiers onto this simple belief. We have learned that people work not only for salaries, but for less tangible returns such as self-realization, job satisfaction, independence, security, prestige, and to give meaning and companionship to their lives. Some researchers say that higher pay may not be the most important of these motives; among higher level employees it may not be very important at all.

One of the results of the tendency of some researchers to stress non-financial incentives is that managers are not always sure what place, if any, money should have as a motivator of performance effectiveness. The myths that have grown up about management compensation as a result of this confusion are well illustrated in a study I conducted recently among 500 managers from all levels of management and from a wide variety of organizations. They were asked whether they agreed or disagreed with five statements that contained assumptions about the psychological aspects of management compensation—assumptions with important implications for the administration of pay.

■ At the higher paid levels of management, pay isn't one of the two or three most important job factors (61 percent agreed).

■ Money is an ineffective motivator of outstanding job performance at the management level (55 percent agreed).

■ Information about management pay rates is best kept secret (77 percent agreed).

■ Managers are likely to be dissatisfied with their pay even if they are highly paid (54 percent agreed).

■ Managers are not concerned with how their salary is divided between cash and fringe benefits; the important thing is the amount of salary they receive (45 percent agreed).

As can be seen, better than 50 percent of managers participating in the study agreed with the first four assumptions, and almost that many agreed with the last.

Recently, research results have begun to accumulate which suggest that all of these assumptions may be partially or completely invalid. Let us therefore examine them more closely.

Historically, we have progressed from the view that man is primarily motivated by economic motives to one that stresses psychological and social needs. This is all to the good; but it may have gone too far. Those who have emphasized the importance of non-economic goods have tended to downgrade the continuing importance of pay. Either they have overlooked it altogether, or they imply that, in our time of general affluence, it is not as important as it used to be. Since experts in "human relations" have shown pay to be relatively unimportant, managers feel they are compelled to play it down too. When the managers in my study were asked how they thought the experts would reply to the statement that pay isn't a major job factor to the higher paid executives, 71 percent said they thought experts would agree. What of themselves? Fewer—but still a majority (61 percent)—of the managers also agreed.

Does this mean that pay should be dismissed as unimportant? I do not think the evidence justifies such a conclusion.

The belief that pay decreases in importance as one accumulates more and more has its roots in Abraham Maslow's theory of a hierarchy of needs. Briefly, Maslow's theory says that human needs are arranged in a hierarchy of decreasing urgency. At the bottom are survival and physical comfort. These are followed by social needs, esteem needs, and finally, needs for autonomy and self-actualization. According to Maslow, once the lower order needs are relatively well satisfied, they become unimportant as motivators, and people turn toward the higher order needs. If it is assumed (as most do who say pay is unimportant) that pay satisfies only lower level needs, then it becomes obvious that once a person's physical comforts are taken care of, his pay will become unimportant.

But I do not believe that pay satisfies only lower level needs. I contend that *pay is a unique incentive—unique because it is able to satisfy both the lower order physiological and security needs, and also higher needs such as esteem and recognition.* Recent studies show that managers frequently think of their pay as a form of recognition for a job well done and as a mark of achievement. The president of a large corporation has clearly pointed out why:

Achievement in the managerial field is much less spectacular than comparable success in many of the professions . . . the scientist, for example, who wins the Nobel prize. . . . In fact, the more effective an executive, the more his own identity and personality blend into the background of his organization, and the greater is his relative anonymity outside his immediate circle.

One form of recognition that managers do receive that is visible and "spectacular" is pay. Pay has become an important indicator of the value of a person to an organization. Thus it is not surprising to hear that one newly-elected company president whose "other" income from securities approximated $125,000, nevertheless demanded a salary of $100,000. When asked why he did not take $50,000, and defer the rest until after retirement, at a sizable tax saving, he replied, "I want my salary to be six figures when it appears in the proxy statement."

It is precisely because pay satisfies higher order needs as well as lower order needs that it may remain important to managers regardless of how large their income is. For example, one recent study clearly showed that although pay is slightly less important to upper level managers (presidents and vice-presidents) than it is to lower level managers, it is still more important than security, social, and esteem needs for upper level managers. At the lower management level, pay was rated as more important than all but self-actualization needs. (See Figure 1)

We can turn to motivation theory to help explain further why pay continues to be important to many managers. Goals that are initially desired only as a means to

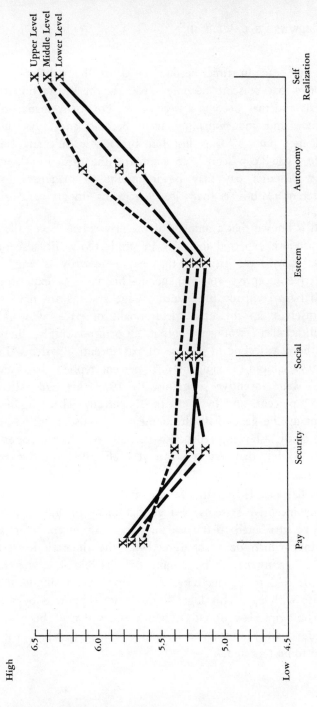

Figure 1—The importance of personal needs varies with the manager's level. *(Left-hand scale numbers are arbitrary.)*

an end can in time become ends in themselves—thus money may cease to be only a path to the satisfaction of needs and may become a need itself. For many managers, money and money-making have become ends. As one manager put it, "It is just like bridge—it isn't any fun unless you keep score." In summary, the evidence shows that although pay may be important to managers for different reasons as they rise, it remains important at all levels.

It is known that a number of incentive plans have failed to produce expected increases in productivity. Because of this, many have assumed that pay necessarily is an ineffective incentive for managers. This view is expressed well by a company president: "Wage systems are not, in themselves, an important determinant of pace of work, application to work, or output." Correspondingly, there has been a decline in the use of pay incentive systems. In a 1935 sample of companies 75 percent replied that they used wage incentive programs. By 1939 this had fallen to 52 percent, and by 1958 to 27 percent. These figures point up the general disillusionment; it is also reflected in my study, showing that 55 percent of the managers sampled felt that pay is not a very effective incentive at the management level.

What has led to the failure and abandonment of so many incentive systems? I feel that many of the failures can be attributed to the use of pay as an incentive in a manner which does not agree with the theoretical basis for expecting pay to be a motivator. The logic is that if pay is tied to productivity, then productivity should increase with pay. This logic seems to be supported by the psychological law of effect, which states that if behavior (productivity) appears to lead to a reward (pay), it will tend to be repeated.

But do incentive schemes designed to relate pay to productivity really follow the law of effect? I believe they do not because typically they are not concerned with *whether the managers see their pay as tied to performance.* Top management is typically concerned only with whether *they* feel pay is tied to performance and not whether other employees feel this way. I have considerable evidence that many managers who work under systems that, according to top management, tie productivity to pay simply do not feel that better work will bring them higher pay.

I recently distributed a questionnaire to over 600 middle and lower level managers in a variety of organizations, all of which purported to use pay as an incentive. The managers were asked what factors determined their pay. The consensus was that the most important ones were training and experience—*not* performance. A look at how their superiors rated them, and their pay, showed that they were correct. There was virtually *no* relationship between pay and rated job performance. How then could they believe in their organizations' incentive programs?

But other data from the same managers did show that pay can be an effective incentive. Those managers most highly motivated to perform their jobs effectively were characterized by two attitudes: (1) They said that their pay was important to them. (2) They felt that good job performance would lead to higher pay. For them the law of effect was in order—pay was a significant reward which they saw as contingent upon performance.

It is not enough therefore to have a pay plan *called* an incentive system. The people subject to the plan must *feel* that it is an incentive and this comes about only when they feel their pay is related to their performance.

In the companies I studied pay actually was not closely tied to performance, so it is not surprising that the managers doubted that it was. But there is still a question of whether actually tying pay to performance will guarantee that employees accept that the relationship holds for them. I feel it is not enough, although it probably is a necessary precondition. Indeed, there is considerable evidence that even workers on piece-rate plans are not convinced that their long-term economic good will be furthered by high productivity. One reason for this is that in order to believe that pay is tied to performance an employee, whether he is a manager or a worker, must have substantial trust in his superior and other members of the organization. Without a high degree of trust, the individual can hardly be expected to believe that his performance will be fairly evaluated and that his long-term economic good will be furthered by performing well. That such trust often is not present, and indeed, that it often is not deserved, is illustrated by the many cases of piece-rate changes and consequent quota restrictions that have occurred to workers in many organizations.

It also seems that for employees to believe that pay is tied to performance, there must be good communication about pay policies and actions. As we will see, secrecy often interferes with these necessary communications.

The unintended consequence of many stock option and bonus plans is to circumvent the problems of establishing trust and good relationships between superior and subordinate by establishing an automatic "objective" reward system. But my feeling is that even "objective" financial reward systems will never be effective under conditions of low trust and poor relationships. This also appears to be true for the many management compensation plans. Many of these management incentive plans (such as stock options) often do more to destroy the perception that pay is based upon performance than to encourage it. They pay off years after the behavior that is supposed to be rewarded has taken place; and the size of the reward given is often independent of the quality of performance.

Two other factors suggest that cash payments may be particularly appropriate now:

■ A recent study found that managers preferred cash payments to other forms of compensation.

■ New tax laws now make it possible to get almost as much money into the hands of the manager through salary as through stock options and other forms of deferred payment.

There is one other reason why incentive plans often fail. They are frequently set up in such a way that earning more money must be done at the expense of the satisfaction of other needs or desires. For instance, if managers are rewarded solely on the basis of the performance of subordinates, they are caught in a bind: on the one hand they want more production, no matter what it costs the total organization; on the other, they want to cooperate with managers in other parts of the organization. Thus, the pay incentive system may set up a conflict system for managers as a piece-rate system often does for blue collar workers.

In summary, the significant question is not whether pay is effective or ineffective as an incentive, but under what conditions it is most effective. Pay can potently motivate good job performance when managers understand that it is being deliberately used to reward, or to extend recognition for, good performance—and when other needs are also met by good and effective work.

We frequently hear that, with money as with peanuts, no matter how much someone gets, he always wants more. And indeed, as demonstrated earlier, pay does remain important, no matter what a man's income. But the conclusion, accepted by 54 percent of those in my study, that managers will remain dissatisfied even if highly paid, does not necessarily follow from this premise.

There is an important difference between how much someone wants to get and what he feels is fair for what he is doing. Individuals tend to strike a mental balance between what they put into their jobs (effort, skill, education, experience, time, new ideas) and what they receive in return (money, status, privileges, etc.). Dissatisfaction comes when an individual feels that what he puts out exceeds what he gets back in the form of pay. He judges the fairness of the balance by comparing it to what other employees, usually co-workers, put out and get back. Dissatisfaction will usually come when one man's pay is lower than that of someone he considers roughly equal or inferior in ability, job level, and performance. But when he gets pay that compares favorably, he will tend to be satisfied. This does not mean, of course, that he would pass up a chance to make more money; it simply means that he feels he is being fairly treated and is not dissatisfied.

A recent study of over 1,900 managers shows that managers can be, and in fact frequently are, satisfied with their pay. They were first asked to rate on a scale (from one to seven) how much pay they received for their jobs. Next they were asked to rate how much pay they *should receive*.

As can be seen from Figure 2, which presents the results for the presidents who participated in the study, those paid high in relation to other presidents were satisfied. For this group ($50,000 and over), there was no difference between what they said they received and what they thought they should receive. But those receiving less than other presidents said there was a substantial difference between what their pay should be and what it was. The same results were obtained at each level of management down to

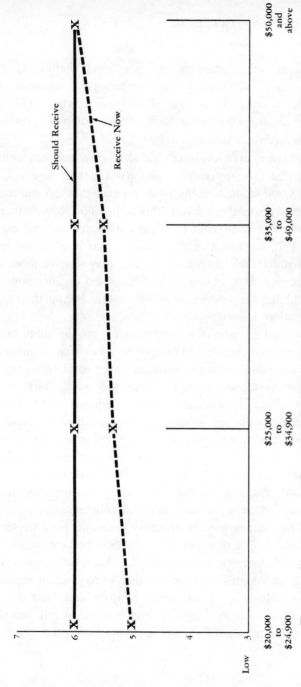

High

7

6 — X

$20,000
to
$24,900

Should Receive

Receive Now

X — $25,000
to
$34,900

X — $35,000
to
$49,000

X — $50,000
and
above

5 — X

4

Low
3

Figure 2—Are company presidents satisfied with their pay? Yes, if they earn $50,000 or more per year. Otherwise, no. (Left-hand scale numbers are arbitrary.)

and including foremen. At each level the highly paid were quite satisfied; it was the low paid managers who were dissatisfied. In fact, highly paid foremen ($12,000 and above) were better satisfied than company presidents who received less than $50,000.

There is even evidence that some managers can and do feel that they receive too much pay for their positions. Of the 1,900 studied, about 5 percent said they got too much. They apparently reached this conclusion by comparing themselves with other managers. Although the percentage is small, the fact that this feeling exists at all is evidence that individuals do not always feel they deserve more and more pay. It is also evidence that some organizations are not doing the best possible job of distributing their compensation dollars.

It may be wise for companies to consult subordinates and peers when considering pay raises for a manager. Giving a high salary to someone other employees consider a poor performer can have several bad results. First, it can cause dissatisfaction among other managers who are good performers but get no raise. Good performers will never be satisfied with their pay under such circumstances. Second, and most important, a raise to a poor performer is a signal to other managers that pay is not really based on merit—an attitude that can destroy any motivational impetus created by an otherwise well-administered compensation program.

The most commonly accepted axiom of good personnel practice is that management pay should be kept secret. (77 percent of my sample accepted it.) Many organizations go to great lengths to maintain this secrecy. Information is frequently kept locked in the company safe, and the pay checks of top management may receive special handling so that the salaries are not known even to the personnel manager.

The reason typically given is that secrecy helps to reduce dissatisfaction: what managers don't know won't hurt them, since they can't make invidious comparisons. But this reasoning is false; they make the comparisons anyway. What has not been clear in the past is to what extent secrecy affects the accuracy of the guesses they make upon which to base their comparisons.

Trying to gather some evidence about the effects of secrecy, I recently conducted an attitude survey. The following specific questions were investigated:

—Is there a tendency for managers to feel that there is too large or too small a difference between their pay and that of their subordinates and that of their superiors?

—Is a manager's satisfaction with the size of the difference between his pay and that of his superior or subordinate related to his satisfaction with his overall pay level?

—Do managers have an accurate picture of the pay of other managers?

The questionnaire was distributed to 635 middle and lower level managers in four private companies and in three government organizations. Responses were received from 563 managers (response rate of 88.7 percent). The four private companies were in widely different industries. They had in common secrecy policies about management pay. The managers in the government organizations also had widely varied jobs, ranging from managing liquor stores to soil conservation. These government organizations did make some information about their general pay rates available to managers, but the salary of each was confidential. Because of the wide variety of organizations sampled, and because of the high response rate, the results of this study should have relevance for a great number and variety of organizations.

The questionnaire had two parts. One asked the managers to estimate average yearly salaries of managers in their organizations at their own level, one above, and one below. (Actual average salaries were revealed to me by the organizations.) The second part asked the managers to indicate how well satisfied they were with their own salaries. They were also asked whether there was too much or too little difference between their own pay and that of their superiors and their subordinates.

The results clearly showed that in addition to often feeling that their own pay was too low, these managers felt that the pay of both subordinates and superiors was too close to theirs. They apparently felt that the pay scales in their organizations are too compact—not enough separation existing between the salaries at different management levels. Thus, regardless of whether a manager looked upward or downward he would be dissatisfied with what he saw. (He was slightly more apt to be dissatisfied if he looked downward, feeling that his subordinates were too close behind him.) When he looked below, or alongside at those at his own level, he apparently felt that their high rates of pay showed he was not sufficiently appreciated.

Actually, however, he underestimated what his superiors were getting and overestimated the pay of subordinates and peers, thereby misunderstanding his own position in relation to them. One-third of the managers overestimated the annual pay of their subordinates by more than $1,000. The managers answering the questionnaire did not have a clear picture of the real situation—secrecy had kept them from it—and so much of their dissatisfaction was not only unnecessary but based on erroneous guesses. Interestingly, government managers were consistently more accurate than the private managers—because they had more accurate information.

What were the effects of these distorted pictures on job

performance and satisfaction? Since managers judge fairness by comparisons, and they estimated peer and subordinate pay too high, it followed that they felt their own salaries to be too low. Obviously, one effect of secrecy may be to increase dissatisfaction.

Secrecy may also contribute to dissatisfaction and lowered incentive when used by an executive to avoid telling subordinates what he really thinks of their work. Frequently a manager, distributing raises, gives some employees more than others because of greater improvement. However, if he tells each that he has given as much as he could, he implies that he is in general satisfied with their performances. The amount of increase is not tied in the subordinate's mind to the quality of his effort—the good worker is not sure he is getting more than the poor one, and the poor performer may feel his work is apparently good enough because he got a raise too.

There are other disadvantages to secrecy. Several studies have shown that accurate feedback about quality of work is a strong stimulus to good performance. People work better when they know how well they are doing—in relation to some meaningful standard. For a manager, pay is one of the most meaningful pieces of feedback information. High pay means good performance. Low pay is a signal that he is not doing well and had better improve. Our findings show that when managers don't really know what other managers earn, they can't correctly evaluate their own pay. Since they tend to overestimate the pay of subordinates and peers, the majority of them consider their pay as low—in effect, they receive negative feedback. Moreover, even when this feedback suggests they should change work behavior, it does not tell them what type of change to make. When managers are not doing their jobs well, negative feedback is undoubtedly what they need.

But it gives a false signal to managers who are working effectively. Overall, it may be that because of the rumors and false information that inevitably circulate when pay is secret, then salary information must be public if managers are ever to believe that pay is based upon performance.

If secrecy policies cost so much in job satisfaction and in motivation for effective performance and promotion, it seems only sensible to abandon them. But what type of information *should* be given? Should managers be told what every other manager earns? Ultimately, I think this may be advisable. Initially, organizations that now have strict secrecy policies could start to move in this direction by giving out accurate information about the average or median salary at different levels and for different types of jobs. Managers could also be told the pay ranges for these jobs and they could be told the control points or similar devices that are used to determine their pay. But such limited information should only be a first step toward complete disclosure when the climate of the organization is prepared for it. There is no definitive reason why organizations cannot make salaries public information. It is far better to let managers know exactly how their pay compares with that of other managers than to have them make inaccurate and unfavorable comparisons based upon misinformation.

When any organization is asked how much money it spends on compensation, it usually adds together money spent for salaries and fringe benefits. Union contracts are usually described as providing an x-cents-per-hour compensation "package." But is a dollar spent on cash salary really equal to a dollar spent on life insurance or other fringe benefits? Economically, and in terms of costs to the organization, it seems so; and this is probably why 45 percent of managers sampled believe that managers are not greatly concerned with how their pay is divided.

However, I do not believe that each manager actually regards the component parts of his own compensation this way. Several studies show that some benefits are valued more than others, even though the cost to the company is the same. For example, one study found that most employees strongly preferred hospital insurance to additional pension money, though both cost the organization the same.

The preferences of individuals for different benefits vary greatly, depending upon such factors as age, sex, marital status, and number of children. Older workers value pension plans much more than do younger workers, and unmarried men value a shorter work week more highly than married men, undoubtedly because different needs are salient for them. Managers in one location want certain things, in another they want others—which indicates that an organization may need different benefit packages in different locations. They may also have to design different packages for different groups. Indeed, it may be that the optimum solution is to adopt a "cafeteria" compensation program—that is, a plan that would allow every employee to divide his compensation dollars as he sees fit among the benefits offered. Previously, such a program would have been too difficult to be practical; but the computer now makes it feasible.

Cafeteria wage plans would appear to have a particularly bright future among managers who are unfettered by union contracts. Cafeteria wage plans have two additional benefits. First, they allow employees to participate in an important decision about their jobs. Even among managers, opportunities for actual participation (as contrasted with pseudo-participation for morale purposes) are rare enough so that in every situation where participation can be legitimately and reasonably employed, it should be. Second, cafeteria-style wage plans help to make clear to the employees just how much money actually goes into their total compensation package. There are many reports of situations where employees do not even know of the fringe benefits for which their organizations are paying. With cafeteria wage plans this would be virtually eliminated.

What are the lessons to be learned from the recent research on the psychological aspects of compensation practices? I believe the following conclusions appear warranted:

■ Even at the higher paid levels of management, pay is important enough to be a significant motivator of good job performance. However, it will be a motivator only when seen by the managers themselves as tied to performance.

■ Managers can be, and in fact frequently are, satisfied with their pay when it compares favorably with that of other managers holding similar positions.

■ Secrecy policies have significant hidden costs attached to them. The evidence indicates that secrecy may lead to lower satisfaction with pay and to a decreased motivation for effective performance.

■ In order to get the maximum value for money spent on compensation, organizations may have to institute cafeteria-style wage payment systems to allow each manager to select the benefits and the amounts he wants.

Will organizations be willing to make these innovations? This question can be answered finally only five or ten years from now. However, there are at least two immediate reasons for believing that organizations will be slow to change.

First, as one critic has put it, most organizations seem intent on keeping their compensation programs up with but never ahead of the Joneses—in a "me too" type of behavior. Unfortunately, many organizations got badly "burned" when they tried to install piece-rate incentive wage schemes that ignored needs other than money. Once burned, twice shy.

Second, since none of the results of this group of studies offers a miraculous cure for present ills, slow movement may be desirable and necessary. These studies show that there are costs and risks involved. For example, it appears that if companies wish to make the most efficient use of pay as an incentive, they must be willing to improve communications about how pay is determined. They must develop an effective performance appraisal and measurement system. They must have a situation where high trust exists between superiors and subordinates. Finally, they must consider gradually eliminating secrecy about compensation.

Just the action of eliminating secrecy, no matter how well handled, will probably cause problems for some employees. In particular, openness will be difficult for the relatively low paid managers to handle. Others can, legitimately, believe their privacy has been violated.

The same point can be made about tying pay more clearly to performance, or about cafeteria-style wage plans. Any innovation entails costs; but the fact that top management continually questions present compensation systems suggests that innovation is needed and that eventually it will take place.

*January/February 1967*

# Conflict
# in the Executive Suite

ROSS STAGNER

How do major industrial corporations settle high-level conflicts on vital policy decisions? Is money the most important determining factor? Is there usually an internal power struggle, with one faction emerging on top? Are agreements reached through the force of winning personality and superior persuasive powers exerted in tete-a-tete conversations? Or, finally, if nothing else works, does the chief officer simply move in and crack heads until he gets agreement?

All corporations establish policies about decision-making which are supposed to apply across the board to all departments and divisions; they are designed to minimize differences and help settle disputes. However, major disagreements between the heads of divisions can develop over the interpretation of corporate policy.

How do such disagreements, involving executives at the vice-presidential level and higher, get settled? There are

three general theories about it:
- *economic*—higher profits are the final determinant;
- *pressure groups*—insiders fight it out in a power struggle;
- *small groups*—disputing executives discuss and decide matters face-to-face.

Each approach is based on different assumptions about the strategies and goals of corporate leaders.

ECONOMIC. Economists generally make three basic assumptions about corporate in-fighting:
- Decisions will be based on rational economic considerations (short-run or long-run).
- A company functions as a unit—that is, internal dissensions can be disregarded in making major decisions.
- Decisions will be based, finally, on considerations of marginal costs and profits—how much the decision will add to the budget and how much extra it will bring in.

Business, therefore, according to the economists, will, under *normal* circumstances, do what businesses are supposed to do: respond only to economic pressures. In practice, conditions are rarely normal; but this does not alter the validity of the concept, as the economists see it. The theory deals with basic forces, with the way businesses *naturally* operate, without regard for the temporary disruptions of abnormal circumstances.

PRESSURE GROUP. The fundamental concept here is that the firm is not a unit at all, but a collection of pressure groups often pulling in different directions, much as Congress may be regarded as a collection of special interests and blocs. Total action can be taken only when dominant coalitions are formed between groups having a common interest, even if temporary.

This theory assumes that division leaders will be concerned first with the welfare of their own divisions, and only secondly with the corporation as a whole. It also assumes bargaining between these "dukedoms," and the development of "political" solutions based on compromise and exchange of favors.

SMALL GROUP. It is possible to regard five or six vice-presidents or heads of divisions, sitting down together to discuss issues and arrive at decisions, as a small group. In such a case, the decision-making process should reflect the forces that we know apply to small groups, such as effective communication, aggressive persuasion, the effects of personal likes and dislikes, and how competent each participant decides the others are.

In order to determine what executives themselves believe to be the most important factors in decision-making, I interviewed about fifty vice-presidents (or equivalents) in ten major corporations (employing from 2000 to 50,000 persons each) in the eastern United States.

The elements they considered most vital in such choices fell into three major categories which I call *dynamic, cognitive,* and *structural.*

■ *Dynamic* embraces motives and goals that the executives felt were best satisfied by choosing one solution over all others.

■ *Cognitive* refers to the way each executive saw or interpreted the situation.

■ *Structural* means the kind of corporation each belonged to, and its systems of communication and chains of command.

Let us examine each category more fully.

DYNAMIC. The dynamic factor most often cited by executives is, of course, *economics.* In practice, this factor is far more complicated than a simple computation of costs versus profits. One executive, who was just then in the process of spending a million dollars for a new warehouse, said quite frankly that he did not expect it to reduce materials handling costs significantly. "But," he added, "you don't want to live in a quonset hut *all* your life." Another, in a different industry, said of a particular decision, "Profitability had nothing to do with it."

On the other hand, in many companies cost figures were determined with considerable care before decisions were made. Amortization of new machinery, for example, might have to be accomplished within four years to be acceptable. This amounts to a 25 percent return on investment, which, to a layman like myself, seems pretty steep. However, the companies setting this high figure apparently had a serious problem of rapid technological change. More stable industries showed figures as low as 6 percent for recouping costs, and this might give them more economic leeway in making decisions.

Further, it became clear in the course of the interviews that cost figures, no matter how precise they seemed, should not be taken at face value. As one man put it, "The salesmen handling this line wanted to have unit cost data. I opposed giving it to them, partly because they might unintentionally reveal it to a competitor, but more because these cost figures are *in some respects artificial* and would easily be subject to misinterpretation." While he declined to elaborate, the implication was strong that actual costs were lower than those listed.

It should be remembered that even under the best circumstances, costs—and profits—are often difficult to compute, and especially to project, accurately. They depend on such fluid concepts as estimated depreciation, allocation of overhead, anticipated volume (and sales), and the hope that no sudden or hidden fluctuations in labor or material costs will occur. Further, there is the old argument between short-term and long-term profit: for instance, the man who planned the new warehouse may well have felt that although no *immediate* return could be expected, it would save costs *in the long run*. In short, the economic yardstick contains so much rubber that it might well be stretched to cover many personal and power considerations, all claiming to be economic.

*Power* is a major dynamic factor. Certain high-level executives tried to maintain their own power or the power of their divisions with some open disregard for profit. For example, in one company it was proposed that three new installations be built, two in the USA and one in western Europe, each costing $5,000,000. The heads of the English and the French subsidiaries got into a feud over which would get the European unit. After considerable negotiating, the executives in the American parent company decided to put *one each* in France and England. This kind of solution is, of course, simple if you have enough money.

In another case, two executives differed vigorously over who should get control of a new computer installation. Finally, two sections were set up, one to be involved in routine computer use, and one to concentrate on planning for future applications of automatic data processing. To no one's surprise, one section was put under Vice-President Smith and the second under Vice-President Jones.

Generally, executives would not talk about jealousy and personal feelings. However, one man did tell me that he protested the promotion of a colleague to executive vice-president; while he did not succeed in blocking the promotion, he did arrange to continue reporting directly to the president, not through the new executive vice-president. I was not surprised when informed later by others that he had expected to get the promotion himself.

Divisional heads will resent and often resist any change in central office policy which makes their units look less profitable. They become personally involved with the welfare of their divisions. One man told me: "Take Division A. They have increased their billings by 500 percent in four years, but have shown very little increase in profit. Naturally, they're critical of our pricing policy because they think it makes them look bad." Central office control over divisions may bring an intense struggle for power: "Conflicts are particularly acute with Division X, which was until recently an independent company and a competitor of what is now the larger portion of the merged corporation."

For the most part, however, overt "factionalism" in top management is muted. It is perhaps significant that in the only company in my survey where two vice-presidents were known leaders of competing factions, one was fired before the year was out. This suggests that covert power struggles are permissible but open conflict is settled by eliminating the weaker.

A few concerns indicated that *political* and *public relations* factors sometimes outweighed costs. One man said: "We could cut prices low enough to bankrupt our nearest competitor and still operate at a profit, but we are not going to do so because we do not want to get involved in an antitrust action." Another said: "We kept our Canadian plant going when it would have been more profitable to close it, because *we did not want to lay off these employees*." However, another man in the same firm diagnosed the major reason as *fear of political repercussions* in Canada if the plant had been shut down. It was clear that non-economic considerations, at least in the short run, determined policy. (In the long run, of course, political repercussions—or antitrust action—may determine whether a plant survives at all.)

COGNITIVE. Decisions are also greatly affected by the fact that different people see and interpret the same things differently. These are the *cognitive factors*.

Depending on their jobs, and their personalities, executives will emphasize different elements in the same collection of information. Particularly, staff officials and operating executives have contrasting approaches. The most frequent example is the statement by production men that market researchers always overestimate demand for a proposed new product. Arguments may get to be so intense that some chief executives will even hire outside consultants in order to get an objective view of what is happening in their own companies.

Many executives I interviewed recognized the importance of learning to see things in a common frame of reference. Communication is especially easy if executives share a common background. One man commented, "When our chief executive was an engineer, I could communicate fairly easily. But our new chief is an economist, and I can't get through to him as well. I think a man will unconsciously listen more closely to someone with a background and experience like his own. Even though I've known this man for thirty years, he listens more to the officers who are economists."

Almost all respondents agreed that socializing with other executives outside of office hours improved communication and mutual understanding. As it happened, however, there was considerable friction in some firms where socializing was especially frequent. It may well be—as some people have said about husbands and wives—that real understanding may just make things worse.

In one company the opinion was expressed that "it takes a man about five years to become a member of the management team." In a way this corresponds with the statement by E. J. Cordiner, president of General Electric, who wrote not long ago that "The board of directors made me president of the company in 1950, but it took four years before the organization gave me the same honor." Decision making—and acceptance—do not occur automatically. There must be a process of learning, and of breaking old biases and ties, before new habits of perception and action are established.

STRUCTURAL. Chief executives differ markedly in the style with which they participate in the communication process and dispute settlements.

Some will call in all of the executives affected and try to get an open expression of divergent points of view. Generally, the man using this technique is cautious to conceal his own preference until he has gotten all opinions. Otherwise there will be a rush to get on his bandwagon and the problem may suddenly be "solved unanimously."

Another pattern involves calling in the principals in a dispute separately, exploring the problem, and later announcing a decision. This seems to have the advantage of avoiding open controversy and facilitating face-saving devices. Nevertheless, it often upsets the "losing" executive, who implies that he has not gotten a fair deal.

Many firms use the technique of having the executive vice-president rule, leaving the president uninvolved so that appeals to him are still possible. If no one screams, the decision is allowed to stand.

My comments about the effectiveness of these techniques must be impressionistic. Nonetheless, it seemed clear that satisfaction was more wide-spread when more executives participated in a discussion of a problem. When the chief executive talked privately first with one, then with another vice-president, then laid down the decision, minimum satisfaction resulted. This impression may be in part caused by the vocal discontent of those whose solution was rejected. But it would, nonetheless, seem compatible with the findings of research on small groups—the man who has his preference argued down in open discussion before an "impartial" president will at least feel that he has taken part in the decision making process.

The most potent, and most often mentioned, influence toward accepting a non-preferred solution was the power of the chief executive. Regardless of widespread talk about decentralization and democratization, the boss is still the boss. "When we could not agree, we took it to the president and he settled it," was a typical report. Thus, the mode of conflict resolution by appeal to a higher authority is widely accepted in industry.

Centralized power also exerts influence indirectly. Controversies between divisions were occasionally played down because of concern for front office reaction. "It would not be good policy to embarrass another division," said one respondent. "It might have a bad effect on a man's chance for promotion."

The chief executive sometimes elects to function as a *mediator* rather than as an arbitrator. One vice-president described the chairman of the board as "a man who would bring two division managers into his office and ask them questions until they arrived at an acceptable conclusion." It is possible that some of the questions revealed the preference of the chairman and involved an implied coercion, but it was clear that no direct pressure was utilized.

Muzafer Sherif has laid great stress, in his recent writings, on the importance of a *superordinate* goal as the most important element to bring about cooperative behavior.

Certainly the sharing of common goals—the profitability and viability of the corporation for instance—favors compromise rather than last-ditch defense of preferred solutions. *Viability* means continued position, power, and prestige to the executive, *profitability* means more personal economic advantage. Most vice-presidents own stock in their corporation. They thus have an interest in corporate profits as well as in divisional power.

Another common type of pressure is similar to what we find in small-group discussion situations. One company reported a practice of having each vice-president bring in his budget for the following year, present it to the policy committee, and defend new expenditures. After all had done this, the requested sums were totaled and compared with estimated income. Since these never balanced, the executive vice-president would then ask everyone to go back and shave down his requests. Men who did not accept significant reductions were subjected to pressure from the group to conform. This did not always work; indeed, in some cases the group agreed that certain expansions were justified and necessary. However, the technique militated against "empire building."

Are vigorous, aggressive, persuasive individuals more likely to "win" controversies than less colorful persons? The consensus was negative. Two executives estimated that such personalities might be effective 20 percent of the time, but in 80 percent of the cases power of the division or status in the company would decide the issue. All respondents agreed that it would be rare for a persuasive man in a lower echelon to win out over a less fluent but higher placed objector.

Personalities do affect decision-making to some extent—but in a negative way. The individual who is unpleasant and irritating to his colleagues is cut out of the communications networks, becomes uninformed and so loses effectiveness. An example: "One divisional manager is technically very competent, but he is blunt and often actually obnoxious. People try to schedule meetings *when they know he cannot attend.*" It is hardly surprising that this individual complained about poor communications in his company.

Over-all, what conclusions can we reach about decision-making among executives?

I cannot be sure without more evidence, but my strong impression is that the effectiveness of pressures to bring about an agreement in decision-making rank in the following order: first, the *power of the chief executive;* second, *shared goals* such as *profitability* of the company; third, *pressure from fellow executives* as a kind of group conformity process; and fourth, *persuasive pressure* by one individual upon another (not reinforced by status differences).

Although a few decisions were based on purely economic considerations, I found that the vast majority were determined in whole or part by these other factors. This would seem to give support to the picture of the corporation as a collection of pressure groups trying to arrive at compromise solutions.

*January/February 1966*

# Taking Over

ALVIN W. GOULDNER

The study of succession—of the passage from an old to a new leader—is as old as history. Indeed, much of history *is* the story of succession. Political scientists and historians have written about succession in high places, long recognizing that the replacement of an old ruler—a king, a dictator, or a president—by a new one, is often accompanied by a crisis. Witness, for example, the Spanish, the Polish or the Austrian wars of succession and the English War of the Roses. And today much of the turmoil in the newly liberated colonial states is due to problems involved in the transfer of power in societies where law and tradition are not yet strong enough to bind the new leaders.

Succession is so important that the forms of government themselves may actually be defined, at least partly, by the kinds of succession they employ. "Democracy" itself can be thought of as a form of succession to the highest office in which the choice is made by popular selection, with guaranteed rights and protection to those replaced, and with the changeover occurring in a more or less peaceful and orderly manner.

Succession, however, is not a problem only for crowns and courts. For leaders come and go in all groups everywhere and on all levels within any group. It is not only Presidents that get voted out but so, too, do wardheelers and city councilmen. It is not only the Chancellor of the University who may decide that he's had enough, but so can the head of the physics department or, for that matter, the man who is chairman of the University's parking committee. It is not only the head of the entire company who can have a massive heart attack but, so too, can the head of the janitorial staff. And the problems of succession are much the same no matter the echelon on which succession occurs. Succession involves us all and takes place about us all the time. It is as inexorable as change and it is as certain as the mortality of men.

The life of men is uncertain—however much we take it for granted and pretend that we are eternal—and the precariousness of men born of their mortality has organizational consequences. In one study of big business executives, for example, it was shown that some 30 percent of successions were caused by death. However trite, however familiar, nothing is more deserving of repetition: men are mortal. The organizations men create must be made of sterner stuff; they must somehow protect their continuity despite the attrition, the turnover—the humanness—of men; otherwise they would quickly go under. And organizations have been set the job of surviving despite the perishability of persons.

One of the basic ways in which this is done is to develop *routines* of succession, so that leadership is passed along from the old man to the new, from the predecessor to the successor, with as little anxiety, disruption and commotion as possible. One way this can be done is through the development of a clear set of *rules* of succession which are acceptable to the group. To the extent that these point unambiguously to the man next in line—the "heir apparent," the crown prince, or vice-president—they make for a smooth transition in power. The group begins to orient itself to the heir apparent, to observe his foibles, to sidle up to and make themselves known to him, to develop expectations concerning his behavior, if and when he should ever take over. The point here is not only that someone is designated as next in line but, rather, that there is a standard and acceptable *procedure* for determining who is to succeed.

It is possible, however, that even though the rules of succession are unclear or doubtful that, nonetheless, the *person* of the heir apparent is not. If someone is specifically appointed as "understudy" for a leader, the group at least knows in advance who will take charge in the event of a change; they will have that much security even if they are not particularly fond of the successor or of the arrangements that led to his designation. If the group is not to flounder when its leader leaves or dies, a new leader must replace him and the sooner the better; the new leader may be specifically designated in advance as the "understudy" or there must at least be clear-cut and acceptable rules for selecting the successor such, for example, as the rules of an election.

Succession is a two-sided process; it involves a great opportunity and a great danger for an organization. On the one side, succession allows an organization to make new adjustments to festering internal problems and new adaptations to its changing environment. Succession can be a creative moment in the life of an organization, permitting it to revitalize and redirect itself. On the other side, succession can also be full of anxiety and a critical moment in the life of an organization, for it carries with it the threat that old familiar policies, arrangements and faces are subject to change.

Succession often brings anxiety and tension to the old subordinates. They fear that the new broom may really sweep clean. They wonder and worry whether the successor will upset old routines and disturb old privileges and positions.

Studies by Robert Guest and myself suggest that if the subordinates liked the predecessor, and liked the way he worked with them and the organization, they will be more anxious about a change. If they disliked him, they will be less anxious and, indeed, may even be pleased.

Moving a man into a position of any importance involves not one but a series of reverberating shifts and successions. The successor who fills one vacancy himself creates a second somewhere else; filling this creates a third vacancy. In short, one succession breeds another.

The truth is we never hire an individual successor, for back of each man hired is an entire group—a "shadow" group. It is only the conventions and myths of our hiring system that require we pretend to be hiring isolated individuals. For when we hire an executive not only does he bring with him his family but—if he has any bargaining power at all—he will usually bring along part of his old work group with him. Indeed, there are some people whom he takes with him as he goes from job to job and city to city.

A man has lived in and was part of a group before he was hired as someone's successor and when he moves he will often want to bring "his own people"—those he knows and trusts, along with him. Indeed, a successor's effectiveness, the very qualities that made him attractive in the first place and brought him into the new job, may derive from the performance of the group organized around him. When James E. Webb was first appointed director of the newly created NASA, he reported that he "came in naked"— meaning that he had not brought in "his own people" with him.

Even a successor formally committed to following his predecessor's programs and policies—as is the vice-president of the United States who succeeds at the death of a president —often very quickly changes the men in positions closest to him. It was not long after President Truman came to power that the Roosevelt cabinet underwent major change. President Johnson succeeded President Kennedy at a time of strong pro-Kennedy feeling and shortly before an election year. Nevertheless, some changes have already been made, and more may be anticipated if Johnson is re-elected.

In many ways the successor, especially if he comes from outside the organization, is a stranger and alone. He is a stranger to that particular job; he is a stranger to the inside information he may need. He is usually a stranger socially —he may not know the men, their first names, their wives, their personal troubles, or their special quirks which may affect their decisions and work. Until the successor can gather his own team around him, his subordinates often have it in their power to frustrate him and perhaps eventually defeat him. And they are more likely to do so if they liked his predecessor, resent him, and question his right to the position. On the other hand, the fact that a successor has fewer friends and fewer ties to the old ways than his predecessor gives him a freer hand to make changes in the policies and men around him.

The key to the success or failure of the successor is very often found in the cooperation—or resistance—of the "old lieutenants." These men have been the cronies and the proteges of the predecessor. They have invested important parts of their working lives in older policies and in the organization. They still possess great power, influence and inside knowledge with which to fight any threat to their positions. My own researches clearly indicated that if the successor, through ignorance or intention, failed to honor the informally privileged positions of the old lieutenants, they would resist. Their attitudes toward the successor are vital in shaping the attitudes of the organization as a whole; they can, and often will, mobilize the sentiment of the rank and file against him, or for him.

A successor who does not at the start gain some support from the old lieutenants will find himself in trouble. He may find his orders sidetracked or sabotaged, his sources of information unreliable or scarce, his mistakes magnified, compounded, and "inadvertently" made known to the main office.

We must not, however, feel too sorry for the successor. If a man's succession entails a promotion, it is obvious that people in powerful places like or respect him. Once again, it needs to be said: no successor—whether he is moving up or down in the world—goes by the name of Robinson Crusoe. If he is going down, be assured, someone is greasing the skids; if he is going up, there are—with equal certainty —some who are helping to pull and to push him up. As the folk wisdom of an earlier generation said of the loyal little woman and her helping hand, the sociologist today might say: Behind every successful (or unsuccessful) man stands a loyal (or disloyal) coterie.

Successors are not chosen merely because they happen to

want the job, or even because they are the most qualified for it. For many are called but few are sponsored. Those finally chosen as the successor are sponsored by men powerful in the organization, by men who may have followed and supported their careers in the systems ever since they came into it. The decisive battle for a succession is more often won or lost by opposing sponsors than by their candidates. The successor may be the instrument and the weapon of the victorious faction in an internal struggle—and the process by which a successor is at last appointed is often a lengthy struggle between contending factions who are supporting different candidates.

The successor is not a self-made man any more than he is a self-born man and when he comes into his new office he comes as a man in debt. The successor bears obligations toward his sponsors and toward whatever purposes they had hoped to accomplish by pressing for his appointment. His sponsors will not usually be long in letting him know what these are; they will "brief" him, defining the organizational situation as they see it. Since the successor knows that his sponsors have power over him—and in any case he feels a natural gratitude toward those who have helped him— the successor will pay close attention to their views and conception of the situation. They may want him to resist threatened changes and stay put; or they may want him to be the instrument of changes they feel to be long overdue. In either event, the successor will soon know what his sponsors expect of him.

Whether a successor came from within the organization or was brought in for the job tells a good deal about what he will do and what his sponsors expect of him. In a study by Richard O. Carlson, superintendents chosen from inside a public school system were contrasted with those brought in from outside: An insider is committed to the familiar. It will be expected of him; habit and experience will incline him toward it; he will be given little leeway to go in any other direction .... The outsider is practically committed to change. He has probably been brought in for this reason. He has fewer ties to the old ways of doing things and to the people who have done them. He has more interest in the advancement of his personal career and ideas . . . since he gets more pay than an insider would, he usually carries more authority, prestige, and power.

The same distinction holds true, with minor modifications, in all managed organizations.

If a successor is an "inside" man, he may have been either promoted or demoted to the job; if an outsider, he may replace someone promoted—or demoted.

A person demoted to a new position has lost face; his self-image, the way people view him, and his influence have diminished. He will tend to withdraw from social contacts. He will be more apt to run his office from a "distance" by rules and regulations and bureaucratic controls rather than by personal contacts. This may also be a matter of some necessity, since, being a man possibly "on the way down," he may not get full cooperation from subordinates. A man who has been promoted, however, is more likely to get the help he needs. Whether a successor arrives via demotion or promotion is important in determining what he will do —and what he will be allowed to do.

How a successor defines his job, and how he should handle it, depends on his sponsorship and briefing, whether he is an insider or outsider, and whether it constitutes a promotion or demotion for him. His projected program will take one of two basic forms, and the successor will emphasize one of two roles:

*The Change-agent—the place needs "tightening up":* The men must toe the line, work harder, and stick to the rules —there must be more efficiency and less fooling around. For all its manifest virtue, this approach is often the more hazardous and may produce great tension.

*The Caretaker—don't rock the boat:* The successor is there mostly as caretaker, to carry on past practices with few changes, and to keep things going smoothly. This usually produces less tension, since even if subordinates dislike "the old ways," they were familiar with them.

Subordinates can be friendly or unfriendly toward a successor, and what they think of him depends very much upon what they thought of his predecessor. The successor's fate at first depends less upon what he does or who he is and more upon how he is seen to compare with "Old So-and-So," his predecessor.

If the subordinates liked the predecessor, they resent and are anxious about the successor. If they did not like him or his methods, the successor will have a far easier time of it.

It may also be suggested as a rule of thumb that the greater the disparity between the subordinates' beliefs and values and those of the sponsor, the greater the conflict between the successor and his subordinates. For the successor will be prone to behave in the efficiency-enhancing ways pleasing to his sponsors but less desired by his subordinates who prefer the familiar old compromises.

The successor who encounters resistance from his subordinates is not long for his job unless he finds some ways of persuading or frightening them into compliance. Among the survival strategies he has at his disposal are the following:

*Pretended friendliness:* The successor can pretend to a sense of intimacy, understanding and friendliness with his subordinates. He is really just one of the boys, working alongside them to get the job done even if he happens to have a more exalted title—in Richard M. Nixon's words shortly after the 1952 elections, he is just an "ordinary fellow who happens to be vice-president."

This tactic will seldom work. No matter how he slices it, the successor is often an outsider, who is not "one of them" at all, and his subordinates know it very well. In any event, he is their *superior;* even if he was one of them before, he is now a different creature.

*Close supervision:* The successor can supervise his new subordinates very closely, try to be everywhere at once, and check everything personally to make sure they do not deceive him. In an organization of any size, this will not work either. The men will resent it, and it can easily degenerate into a vicious cycle in which the harder the successor supervises and spies on them, the less they will follow his orders when he is not actually standing over them. In the end he must be defeated because he simply cannot be everywhere at once.

*Appeasement:* The successor can try to *placate* the old lieutenants by giving them what they think is due them; but they may ungratefully regard this as merely the payment of an obligation and continue in their hostility. The successor can then try to *buy* their support by promotions and new supervisory jobs; but this costs money and may bring him into conflict with supervisors.

*Strategic replacement:* The successor can try to *replace* the old lieutenants, getting rid of the recalcirants and bringing in his own people, those responsible and loyal to him, who will reliably communicate his orders downward into the rank and file. This accomplishes two things at once: it eliminates sources of friction, and replaces them with sources of help. It may also relieve the successor's anxiety to have confidants and friends around him. They may, however, like him, be strangers, unfamiliar with detail, and out of contact with their own subordinates. Until they can master their jobs the successor may still be in trouble. But at their worst the new strategic replacements are better than active enemies and, in time, the successor will have his own loyal corps of lieutenants, and he will no longer need to depend on the old ones.

*Bureaucratization:* Finally the new successor may come to rely more on devices of control that do not require as much personal contact and supervision—on formal procedures, paperwork, rules and regulations. Making supervision a matter of organized impersonal routine allows for more secure and easily defended methods of decision-making, while apparently reducing the supervisor's personal responsibility.

Whether a successor resorts to more bureaucracy depends on whether his subordinates liked his predecessor and on whether he is an insider or an outsider. An outsider will rely more on paperwork and formal procedures, which he may introduce himself; the insider, as in everything else, will be more apt to go along with established procedures. And the successor who follows a much-liked predecessor may meet with the resistance that constrains him to get the job done with the impersonal techniques of bureaucracy.

This article has largely concerned itself with the disruptive effects of succession. Generally speaking, succession causes greatest disruption if:

- the job has great power and discretion (and the organization is highly centralized);
- the predecessor was friendly and highly respected by his subordinates;

- the communication between the previous leader and his subordinates was more personal, less formal, less bureaucratized.

But it is wrong to emphasize one-sidedly the disruptive consequences of succession. Succession is omnipresent; it is necessary and in many cases, however cruel it may seem, it is desirable. For new men mean a new policy and a new chance for the organization. Men become identified with policy, which is not unreasonable since it is they who, often enough, have made it. When change is necessary, to ask them to cooperate wholeheartedly with the people and policies they may have spent their lifetime fighting is simply asking too much of human nature, as we have come to know it. It is also too much to ask of human credulity —for who could trust the old leaders and believe that they had really adopted the new policies?

New men are needed when new policies are to be pursued, men who can believe in the new policies, men who can look to the future without having to justify their past, new men whose very newness dramatizes and symbolizes the changes being made; new men whose very succession to office demonstrates that the organization has made its commitment by turning its back upon those who have labored for the past and investing in those who have publicly staked their futures upon the new policies.

The organization has, of course, been so arranged that, come what may, it will survive—or, at least, such is the hope. No matter how great a man may be in the eyes of his God or his children, he can never be so great in the eyes of his organization that it will lay down its life for him. In the last analysis, a succession has been successful if it has been so adroit that men never notice how close to chaos they have been brought by the succession, and if they never imagine how different things might have been.

It is the moral obligation of the well-managed succession in the well-working organization to bury the dead and to baptize the new with a firm and unfaltering hand, and, suppressing all fear and trembling, artfully to conceal how much the fate of the organization hangs upon the individual.

*March 1964*

# Practical Problems and the Uses of Science

ROBERT K. MERTON/EDWARD C. DEVEREAUX, JR.

What determines whether or not a particular problem, or class of problems, is referred to social research? What considerations affect the demand for applied research? Which conditions foster and which impede research referral?

The demand for applied social research in a business organization is not simply a result of individual decisions separately made about the usefulness of research for each problem. The demand for research is significantly affected by a variety of factors, by changing business conditions and by broad attitudes and beliefs about the efficacy of social research in general.

Research is not an abstraction carried on in a cultural and organizational vacuum. It is done in various concrete social and cultural settings which may be neutral, friendly or suspicious. The discussion that follows explores a few of the conditions that affected the demand for social research during the very early stages of its use in the American Telephone and Telegraph Company. The company's interest in the practical possibilities of social research began to develop as early as the end of the 1920s. Documents from that period and the early 1930s indicate some of the questions that were then being raised:

- How do customers feel about the Company and its service?
- Under what circumstances does the telephone change from a luxury to a necessity?
- What attitudes and beliefs act as deterrents to the use of long-distance telephone service?
- What are the special communication needs of different kinds of businesses?

Applied social research at the Bell Telephone Company, as elsewhere, was a response to practical problems. It needs to be asked, therefore, just what constitutes a practical problem? In general terms, problems are puzzles an individual attempts to solve, but the solution eludes him, at least at first, because he lacks appropriate knowledge or skills. Practical problems are problems that *require* a solution because the individual has some interest in the outcome. Something needs to be done.

At least three essential elements are jointly involved in the emergence of any practical problem:

- a perceived discrepancy between some existing (or future) external situation, on the one hand, and the values or goals of an individual or organization, on the other;
- a feeling of a need for adjustive activity or for corrective action of some sort;
- a "puzzle element"—an awareness of ignorance or doubt about at least some of the facts and relation-

ships believed to be relevant to a decision about what, if anything, should be done.

The existence of such problems is a normal and inescapable circumstance for any individual or for any organization, for there are many discrepancies between external reality and human values or interests. However, discrepancies between external reality and human values or personal interests are not always perceived by those who stand to be affected. Unless all three of the above conditions exist, the individual may experience only a vague uneasiness, a diffuse strain or a mute need; but what he is experiencing is not yet a practical problem.

A problem may emerge as a concern for decision-makers because something has changed and because this change has acted as a catalyst. Various types of change may serve as problem-raising catalysts. Here, however, we propose to discuss only a few of the Bell Telephone materials to explore and expand upon the different ways in which practical problems emerge as a result of only one type of change—a change in the outside objective situation.

The telephone business like others operates in a situation which is continually changing in some respects and is fairly stable in others. If the objective situation were entirely stable, established policies and routines could be allowed to run on indefinitely once their effectiveness had been demonstrated. Since the situation is in a continuous state of flux, however, policies and routines must be reexamined continually. Existing policies must be modified and new policies must be devised to keep the business aligned with ever-changing circumstances.

If effective action is to be taken, these changes must be seen as soon as possible. The old saying that "what you don't know can't hurt you" is no more true of the business firm than of any other organization. It is true, however, that only perceived changes can constitute "problems" in the sense defined above. Yet changes that are not perceived may, and often do, affect the interests of a business.

Continual change virtually forces the business firm, if it does not wish to be caught off guard, to establish and maintain various procedures for routine observations and reports about changes in its environment. These give rise to what we may call "instrument-panel" research. In the context of the social science approach this type of research represents a collective viewing post of the organization; it takes periodic soundings of trends and notes fluctuations in those aspects of the situation that impinge upon the interests of the business. Instrument-panel researches help an organization to become aware of crucial changes in its outside environment which may affect its public relations or marketing activities.

On this topic, one executive observed:

In the advertising field, we are shooting at a fast-moving target. It never stays still. We hope to get from surveys three types of information: (1) some knowledge about where the target is and which way it is moving; (2) what ammunition we should use in trying to hit it; and (3) some indications which would show us how we are doing.

Public opinion is, of course, only one aspect of the changing situation. There are also population movements, fluctuations in the business cycle, constantly shifting markets, changing legal and political arrangements, and varying conditions in the supply and prices of raw materials and labor. These represent but a few of the many social and economic changes about which a firm can use a continuous flow of information.

Instrument-panel studies yield observations that can be plotted as a trend line, and can facilitate the early identification of significant changes. In part, such trend studies simply provide an assurance that all is well. Just as the airplane pilot occasionally checks his instrument panel to make sure that all is running well, so the business executive checks his routine indicators to satisfy himself that there is no change and no problem. The indicators do not, of course, always stay in their "normal" position, and when one or more of them appears to be getting out of line, the pilot or executive is alerted to a new problem. Instrument-panel studies allow company officials to see at a glance how, for example, public attitudes or other important conditions are fluctuating. Such studies may enable threatening changes to be perceived before they can do any damage.

During the depression of the 1930s the number of telephones in use declined sharply. Revenues fell off, but many items of overhead continued much as before. This dramatic change in the objective situation brought into view a variety of problems that were not present during the prosperous period of the 1920s.

Before the depression, for example, the telephone company had concentrated on the essentially technological problems of extending and improving its equipment. Until then, the demand for its product would be taken more or less for granted. During the depression, however, consumer *demand* became the strategic consideration. As attention shifted to the consumer side of the equation, new awareness was born among company executives that very little was actually known about the nature of the demand for telephone service.

The heightened awareness of this newly-important problem produced a flood of ideas about new kinds of information that might be useful. In some cases the questions posed were exceedingly broad; should we undertake an extensive program of basic research into all the problems involved in the psychology and sociology of communication? Others were more narrowly limited, for example: should we attempt to measure the effect of changes in telephone rates upon usage? Some questions like these led to the initiation of actual research projects, but the great majority apparently did not.

We may mention briefly a few studies that were actually carried through: Casting about for new uses of the telephone that might profitably be developed, one of the operating companies decided to explore the use of the telephone for shopping purposes. A survey was made among a sample of customers in a selected community. The pattern of their actual telephone usage was established, and a number of questions were asked about what they perceived to be the advantages and disadvantages of telephone shopping.

The results of this survey were both instructive and useful. It was established, for example, that the inclination among customers to use the telephone for shopping greatly exceeded the facilities of the stores for handling telephone orders. This strategic fact provided leverage for a program. Storekeepers were approached with the idea that it would be good business to provide more clerks and more lines at telephone order desks. Helpful pointers were offered to retailers on the proper training of telephone-order clerks. A series of "shop by telephone" advertisements were based on the information from the survey. The telephone company reported later that these efforts had been very profitable and resulted in a sizeable yearly revenue increase from its small retail accounts in the community.

Another study during this period revealed that 76 percent of the persons interviewed thought that long distance rates were higher than they actually were. This fact, again, provided leverage for a public information program.

Still another study focused upon the nature of the relationships between the people initiating long-distance calls and those whom they called. The knowledge gained in this survey was effectively employed in deciding on advertising approaches to foster the use of long distance facilities for social and family purposes during slack evening hours.

We cannot appreciate why certain of these pioneering studies were carried through during the depression, and why others were not, unless certain general factors are brought into view. Several among these that might be mentioned are:

- Many of the research proposals were too vague or general.
- Policy makers during that earlier period were not yet familiar with the potentialities of research and not yet "sold" on its usefulness.
- Budgets for all items, including research, were sharply curtailed in a time of shrinking revenues.

With the outbreak of World War II, new kinds of problems came into focus and those of the depression receded. The demand for telephone service, and for long distance connections, greatly exceeded existing facilities. As the need to expand telephone services was increasing, the ability to expand was impaired by the acute shortage of many strategic materials and laborpower. Once again, the company's problems became predominantly technological.

But there were also new and special problems of a sociological character, two of which may be mentioned here:

- For the first time in its history, the company found it

necessary to undertake activities designed to restrict the public's use of telephones that were already installed, to persuade people to limit their long distance calls to three minutes, and to make only essential calls.

- The company also became concerned with the public's reactions to such wartime restrictions. Would they be understood and accepted, or would they undermine the public's good will and its confidence in the company's skills and abilities?

At the beginning of the war, some company executives felt that social research was now less necessary. This was so in part because furthering the war effort was seen as the organization's major objective and, in part, because it was felt that little could then be done to remedy any problems revealed by social research, given the scarcity of materials and manpower. Yet if such considerations restricted social research, others led to the conduct of certain researches.

By 1944, for example, the backlog of unfilled orders for new phones was mounting and it was uncertain when they could be filled. What effect would this wait have upon public attitudes toward the company? How could the public be made to understand and to tolerate these unavoidable delays? Concern with these problems had led certain of the company's executives to propose that the social research group develop and proceed with a survey of the public's feelings.

At the same time, the War Production Board—charged with establishing and administering wartime priorities—also became interested in the backlog problem and considered conducting research on public attitudes toward the existent regulations and priorities for allocating phone services. When the WPB found that the telephone company was planning research in this area, and would be able to include questions of interest to the federal agency, the WPB abandoned the idea of a separate research project.

This episode suggests two other general conditions affecting an organization's readiness to accept and pursue plans for social research:

- whether or not these plans are supported by executives highly placed within the organization;
- whether other, outside, related interests will find the research results acceptable and of value.

It is quite clear, then, that the fate of research proposals does not depend only on the specific problems with which they deal. The decision to accept or table them is influenced also by the general attitudes toward research and by other conditions prevalent within the company.

As the telephone company's experience during the depression and the war suggests, the demand for social research is stimulated when an organization's external situation changes. Change brings with it new kinds of problems, the solution of which requires new kinds of information. Such changes must, however, be visible before they can be identified as problems requiring new information and correctives. These changes can be recognized either through the organization's internal records of operations—as they were during the depression—or through special instrument-panel studies. The function of social research, then is not simply to supply information useful in remedying problems already known— it serves also to make the problems known.

*July/August 1964*

# How Scientific Management Thwarts Innovation

VICTOR A. THOMPSON

America, in the year of 1968, is rapidly bogging down. Unless the big federal agencies that have the funds to tackle major domestic problems can come up with some thoroughgoing social innovations, it seems we must give up the dream of the Great Society and resign ourselves to a permanent state of war between the haves and have-nots. Unless the State Department and the President's advisers can devise some new approaches to foreign policy, we may well be condemned to an endless series of wars like the war in Vietnam. But the depressing fact is that the atmosphere in the federal bureaucracy is not at all conducive to framing new policies. And what's even worse, the style of administration in government is moving away from, not closer to, a climate that encourages innovation.

This is a serious charge. I will support it here by reviewing some of what social scientists have learned about the kind of organizational atmosphere that encourages innovation, and then by examining the federal bureaucracy in the light of these findings.

An innovation is really a lucky shot in the dark. All the searcher has to begin with is a general idea of what the problem is and some notion of its components. And even this knowledge is not certain. In the course of his search, the would-be innovator sometimes finds out that he was wrong about the nature of the problem, that some of the components he thought were crucial were really not so important, and that factors he had never considered were of very great importance. The solution he is searching for is, of course, unknown, but he may think he knows the general type of solution that will work.

We don't really know, for example, why ghetto children don't learn much in school. We suppose that racial segregation, crowded classrooms, class differences between teacher and pupil, and the clash between the culture of poverty outside and the middle-class culture inside the schoolroom all have something to do with it. We may be right or wrong about any of these elements and there are surely others that we haven't yet found. What's more, we don't really know what outcome we want. Is it desirable for Negro or Puerto Rican schoolchildren to be stripped of the distinctive features of their own cultures in order to fit more easily into a white, middle-class, standard-English-speaking world? Is it our goal to send the entire school population on to college, or is there some mixture of educational end-points the school system should aim at? What kind of mixture?

At the beginning, at the totally uncertain stage of the problem, all approaches are of equal value because they all generate large amounts of information at relatively small cost. The unpromising approaches can be quickly spotted and weeded out before they become very costly. The new knowledge must be quickly and freely communicated, however, if this shotgun approach is going to yield results. All forms of suppression, from competitive suspicion and secrecy to an insistence on "going through channels," must be ruled out. What is needed is flexibility, pluralism, multiple approaches—exactly what a budget-conscious Congressman or an efficiency expert in a corporation would call duplication or "overlapping."

When investigators actually examine firms that have successful records of innovation, they find a situation very different from the traditional model of the taut ship. They find what, in an innovative organization, is called "slack"—uncommitted resources of personnel, finance, material, and motivation. Although we don't understand exactly how slack increases innovation, the fact that it does is well established. Perhaps the embarrassment of unused resources leads to the search for something worthwhile to do with them. Or perhaps a use is found for them simply because they are there.

When there is slack, the psychological risk of new ventures is reduced: The possible loss of uncommitted resources is less painful than the loss of resources that are already earmarked for a specific use. Like the rich gambler who can afford to lose, the executive who has many uncommitted resources at his disposal will play a riskier game for higher stakes than the one whose resources are so limited that he must play to minimize loss.

For example, rich farmers are the ones who make

agricultural innovations. Farmers who are just scraping by, however low their productivity, will stick to the tried methods. Progressive school systems are generally found in wealthy suburbs, not in the working class or poor neighborhoods of the city. And diverse approaches combined with a fairly loose organizational structure have produced a high innovative payoff in industry, too: The two firms that have made the most successful innovations in the manufacture of jet engines, Pratt & Whitney and Rolls Royce, are pragmatic, trial-and-error decision-makers. Neither firm is set up in a rigid, top-down, comprehensive problem-solving style. Innovation in the aluminum industry, rare when the giant Alcoa corporation dominated the field, increased after 1945 when additional companies entered the field and broke Alcoa's monopoly.

Now that we have looked at the general conditions that promote or inhibit innovation, and considered some examples, let us examine the federal administration as an organization in which innovation may—or may not—take place.

In the last 20 or 30 years, social science has invaded the field of administration, but the invasion has largely by-passed the area of public administration. Behavioral scientists have been invited to work in private organizations, not public ones. The study of public administration is still concerned mainly with budgeting, personnel, operations and methods—just as it was 30 or 40 years ago.

This is the traditional milieu in which most people now in charge of the federal administration were trained, and their administrative practices are the product of this background. Thinking, planning, and decision-making are centralized and separated from doing. Decisions are made by the man at the top, advised by a few trusted staff aides. The rest of the organization only implements these decisions. In the Defense Department, for example, basic decisions are made at the top, often without consultation and even against the advice of the staff. Those who are opposed—like General Curtis LeMay and Admiral David Anderson—are eliminated.

My own impression is that the morale at the Pentagon under these conditions is quite low. People who disagreed seriously with Secretary Robert McNamara usually left the Department, and there is no reason to suppose that the trend will be reversed under Clark Clifford. Major General W.J. Sutton, Pentagon head of the Army Reserve, testified at a Congressional subcommittee hearing that he had not been consulted about merging the Army Reserve with the National Guard, and added that he was opposed to the move. But, he affirmed, he would support his superiors' decision. "I've been a good soldier for 40 years," he said, "and I'm going to continue that record." Evidently, in the military, the good soldier is still the yes man.

This hierarchical system is not limited to the military. When a Senate Judiciary Subcommittee questioned Internal Revenue Service agents as to why they broke the law by breaking and entering and by wiretapping, one agent answered: "Anything that had been asked, I would have done it." Another one said he would break laws "if my superiors told me to." It is perhaps unfair to point out that this behavior is a regression from the organizational behavior standards expressed during the Nuremberg war trails.

Now, in the absence of social science, *non-social*

science has naively invaded the field of public administration. The physical sciences all have models that unify
their fields, define the important problems, provide the
criteria for their solution, and provide examples of
"good" scientific practice. With such an intellectual
apparatus, scientists achieve a high level of success in
solving problems. But many of them do not realize
how easy it has been made for them. They are presented
only with solvable problems, and their "solutions" are
only solutions with reference to the single set of conventions in the field. There is no pluralistic babble of
voices to challenge their successes and impugn their
motives. As C.P. Snow has said, natural scientists—
isolated from the laity both by tradition and by education—become optimists, imbued with the idea of scientific progress and the related notion that science can
also solve social problems. It is from this background
that the current wave of "scientific management" has
arisen.

This is not the first appearance of scientific management on the organizational scene. In an earlier day,
Frederick Taylor and his followers developed a brand
of scientific management that caught the fancy of industry. But as anyone who has seen *The Pajama Game*
will remember, the rigors of the Taylorite time-study
men were kept in bounds by the militancy of organized
labor. And the well-known findings at the Hawthorne
works of Western Electric, which showed how many
complex and intangible factors enter into the question
of why some workers are more productive than others,
also exerted some restraint on the scientific managers.

Today there is a resurgence of the scientific-management mystique. This mystique sees the firm as a system
based entirely upon economic rationality. The model

posits a single, overriding goal for the organization and requires managers to spend their time constantly canvassing all available choices, adopting those that add more to the firm's goal than they cost and discarding any that cost more than they add. This model requires a totally hierarchical organization. It tries to avoid human vagaries by mechanizing and programming every possible activity, and attempts to eliminate all overlap or duplication as a waste of resources. It is the opposite of the loose, overlapping structure with plenty of slack, the structure that is most conducive to innovation.

Unfortunately, there are neither militant unions nor many social scientists in the government to keep this new form of scientific management—these new Taylorites—from sweeping the federal bureaucracy. Thus, President Johnson has ordered all federal agencies to switch to a "planning-programming-budgeting" (P.P.B.) system of control. "The new . . . method is an extension of the 'cost effectiveness' approach Defense Secretary McNamara has been using at the Pentagon," explained the *Wall Street Journal*. "This method will require each agency to spell out specific goals and objectives, set forth different methods of achieving them, attempt to measure exactly what results will be achieved for each dollar spent under each method—and project all of this not just for one year but for five years." [See "Government-Wide Budget Planning," by Murray Weidenbaum, *Trans-action*, March 1968.]

Now, every change in government policy is an opportunity for a new group of people to acquire power. The people who have acquired power under the P.P.B. approach to federal administration are the applied mathematicians—the econometricians, operations researchers, computer programmers, and decision theorists. I usually refer to all of them as "econologicians." They are *econo*logical rather than *socio*logical. To them, the scientific study of administration *must* end up as the scientific administration of things, including people.

Sociologist Robert Boguslaw calls this new administrative élite the New Utopians because they make the same mistakes as all utopians before them. They vastly underestimate the complexity of the units with which they deal—people—and they fail to take adequate account of emergent situations. The underlying assumptions of the new P.P.B. system of control illustrate this point. These assumptions are:

■ The organization can be disregarded—only the means-end logical analysis is relevant.

■ The techniques of mathematics and accounting, not of social science, are the basic managerial tools.

■ Human motivation is not problematic; it can be assumed.

■ There is one best way of doing everything.

■ Rationality involves comprehensive analysis of a problem (getting "all the facts"), and a coordinated movement toward a single pre-set group of goals.

■ Social and cultural conditioning are nonexistent or irrelevant.

■ A single ordering of preferences for all social needs is possible, or at least desirable.

■ It is worthwhile to achieve the form of rationality even though the actual content of policy is not rational.

The form of rationality is achieved by making decisions in accordance with defensible formulas—no matter how arbitrary the values assigned to the variables in those formulas.

■ Organizations are flexible; no particular organizational structure has a special claim to continued existence.
■ Acceptance, consensus, or other social and political criteria will not do as measures of achievement. Only criteria that use mathematical forms of measurement are acceptable.

This new management élite uses a very effective technique for acquiring power—showing certain deficiencies in present decision-making that can be remedied only by themselves. A hypothetical case in an instruction manual developed for the Department of Defense and now being foisted on other segments of the Administration reads: "Having only the vaguest conception of what is involved in the installation of a large-scale data processor, Ferris [vice-president for administration] calls in young Wiley, a staff procedures analyst." Obviously econologician Wiley will set vague old Ferris straight, possibly winding up at some future date with Ferris' job. And note the contempt in the following comment: "The board, after piercing questioning and solemn deliberation, authorized Wiley to begin the project."

A favorite technique of the scientific-management group is to examine decisions, discover the rules of thumb that were used to make the decisions, and then look for the assumptions that must underlie such rules. These assumptions are then presented to the decision-maker—and if he is reluctant to accept them, solemnly warns a textbook on operations research, "then he ought to re-examine very carefully his acceptance of the rule of thumb." The same text threatens that "we are facing a period in which reliance on these [rules of thumb] to the exclusion of other ways of managing will leave us in serious trouble." The logical effect of these criticisms, if they are accepted, is to make management dependent upon the new Taylorites.

These new Taylorites assume that management failures usually occur at the point of policy formation. The policies themselves are irrational and thus inadequate, they assume, because not enough math was used in formulating them. I disagree. I believe that most organizational failures occur further down the line. They are the result of insufficient data about the variables—especially the human variables such as worker efficiency—that intervene between the management-decision inputs and the production outputs. These are the very kinds of data in which utopians have always been deficient. And pumping hypothetical, unconfirmed social and psychological "data" into their equations in no way solves the problem.

The lack of firm data is camouflaged by an emphasis on elaborate procedures. The new Taylorites set up their equations so that they can arrive at definite solutions. This makes them look good, like physical scientists. But this scientism has its dark side: The Taylorites' insistence on simple, clear-cut answers leads them to tackle only the problems they *can* solve, not those that *need* to be solved.

When a business or a government agency is under the administration of scientific management, its clients may feel that they are not getting the service they are entitled to. But service to the client—at least as the client perceives it—is not what keeps scientific management in business. Under modern Taylorism, management's performance is judged not by the clients' perceived welfare, but by their *demonstrable* welfare.

And since the managers themselves design the criteria that demonstrate welfare, demonstrable welfare can be counted on to increase.

Where then, under the sway of the new Taylorites, is our federal bureaucracy heading? The reemergence of Taylorism and the "efficiency and economy" of the Johnson administration are being aided in administrative circles by the absence of social science drive—and by the rapid growth of the data-processing industry, dedicated to the promotion of control-oriented management. At first glance, there seems to be little to stop us from hurtling headlong into the dismal future predicted by George Orwell in *1984*. But there are, fortunately, some counteracting forces.

Social systems, like biological systems, have ways of protecting themselves from threats. One way is to disobey or otherwise evade threatening rules or systems. The many inequities of the income tax law, for instance, are tolerable only because people can engage in minor cheating and evasion. If the income-tax system is mechanized to the point where evasion is impossible, it will have to be completely overhauled or it will founder on the citizens' refusal to cooperate. Similarly, even the bureaucrats resist the cost-accounting systems that dominate today's federal bureaucracy. I have no doubt that one of the most intensely pursued activities in Washington today is how to evade P.P.B., or how to manipulate it so that "you can live with it."

Furthermore, in the field of new weapons research and development, the incompatibility of scientific management and innovation is already becoming evident. Whatever one's opinion about management in the Department of Defense, the mecca of neo-Taylorism, it is clear that weapons like the M-16 rifle and the F-111 (TFX) fighter plane have serious flaws. For all the ballyhoo about the managerial revolution that produced them, the hardware itself does not quite measure up. The rifle jams, and the plane crashes.

Finally, despite Taylorism's ideal of top-down managerial comprehensiveness, there is really no such thing. A working organization consists of conflicting claims on available resources, and policy is the result of negotiations and compromises among the claimants. This is as true of the federal bureaucracy as it is of any private firm. What would happen if all the bureaucratic units of government stopped making claims and sat back and waited for Congress to give them their assignments and budgets? Neither Congress, nor the President, nor anyone else could perform such a function successfully.

Of course, the analytic approach to decision-making, the rigid organizational structure, and the top-down chain of command that characterize modern Taylorism can be useful for certain purposes. This approach probably does succeed in cutting costs and increasing efficiency in certain very routine operations. But efficiency is not the final goal of this or any other society. And the assembly-line approach to problem-solving can yield very little in the way of solutions to the really very major dilemmas facing our federal government.

Our federal administration is stuck dead center on basic policy, both foreign and domestic. Although day-by-day administrative puzzle-solving takes place, nothing very creative is going forward. Clearly, our old solutions to the nation's problems no longer work. But with the rigidities of the new Taylorites continuing to paralyze government decision-making, it may be some time before we get the new solutions we so desperately need.

*June* 1968

Ridgidity of Taylovytes – representing scientificism, are staunch in traditionalism which holds us back from creative innovation.

# A Symposium:

# The Innovating Organization

Innovation is the essential ingredient of the 20th century American success story. Henry Ford, the prototype of all its heroes, went out to the woodshed and developed a practical automobile; he created the assembly line that made automobile manufacture profitable; and he made a fortune. In contemporary industry, innovation is still a key to profits. The locale has switched from the woodshed to the research and development department; the innovator is more likely to be a corporation employee than an entrepreneur on his own. But the corporation that can make an attractive new product, or find a cheaper way to make an old one, is still the model of business success. It is no wonder that corporations want to promote innovation. The crucial question is how.

There is no simple way to categorize organizations as "innovative types." To some, the magic words are "basic research." Western Electric has invested heavily in its research subsidiary, Bell Telephone Labs, and been well paid for its efforts; basic research in Germanium crystals at Bell Labs yielded that eminently practical gadget, the transistor. A highly innovative organization like I.B.M., of course, devotes a sizable portion of its resources to research; yet not all its successful innovations hatch according to plan. Arthur K. Watson, vice president of I.B.M., has said that the disk memory unit, the heart of the modern computer, was developed entirely outside regulation channels, a "bootleg project" carried out in secret against management instructions (from "Organizational Lag" by William M. Evan of the Massachusetts Institute of Technology). Some corporations have nothing to show for their investment in research but their shiny laboratories, producing nothing the corporation can use. Successful corporations sometimes think of new ideas because they've nothing more pressing to do with their resources, and desperate firms have responded to competitive threat with innovation.

A few months ago a group of social scientists were invited by the Graduate School of Business of the University of Chicago to try to answer that question. They were sociologists and economists, psychologists and anthropologists, professors of business administration and of political science. They came to Chicago to pool the resources of their various disciplines in an intensive examination of the problems of innovation.

The social scientists at the Chicago seminar hoped to provide some light in the darkness. While no one knows the whole answer to the innovation problem, social scientists know some things about it. There are findings in all the fields represented at the seminar that bear on the question.

The director of the Chicago seminar, Thomas L. Whisler,

professor of industrial relations at the Graduate School of Business of the University of Chicago, is concerned with specifying "The Meaning of Innovative." An organization is innovative, says Professor Whisler, if it is the first to do something that no other organization of its kind has done before. He draws a distinction between innovation and invention: the distinction lies in the difference between the verbs "to use" and "to conceive." An inventor conceives of a new idea; an innovator puts it to use.

*Trans-action* presents a selection of these papers, in edited form. The papers are diverse, sometimes contradictory, certainly not the final word on the subject. They are also fresh, provocative, and highly innovative in how they tackle the problems of innovation.

---

HOW TO PREVENT INNOVATION

*James Thompson*

Let us imagine that in a large organization there is an employee who sees in some routine occurrence a new and unusual meaning. We are, in other words, assuming the basic ingredients for serendipity. My question is, how can we keep serendipity from occurring? I suppose serendipity usually starts with a flicker of an idea, not a full blown interpretation. If that is so, we might be able to prevent it by keeping our employee so busy that he has no chance to elaborate the flicker into an idea.

If the idea reaches the stage of conscious formulation, we can try to deny the employee resources for developing it. A good device for this is a tight budget, although our obstinate worker might ask for a special allocation. If he makes a weak plea, his idea is lost. If he makes a strong plea, we can still defeat him by placing a dodo at the receiving end—someone too preoccupied or too stupid to see merit in the idea. In fact, at every relay point in the organization where the idea must be put across and accepted, we can put in a poor communicator and a poor receiver.

Suppose that, despite these defenses, our discoverer gets the resources to develop his idea and develops it well. Now comes the process of getting it considered for adoption by the organization, and we still have some points of attack. We can sabotage the various relay points again, either by staffing them with dodos or by keeping them too preoccupied to consider new ideas.

If the idea does get on an organizational agenda, we can assign a low priority to it and, failing that, we can create a crisis that rearranges established priorities and keeps the organization preoccupied. If the idea nevertheless comes up for serious consideration, we shift tactics.

First we arrange for underestimation of potential benefits and/or overestimation of difficulties, costs, and dangers. We do this by staffing the decision unit with short-sighted and cautious types. If the decision unit is full of imaginative risk-takers, we might subject it to external pressures for short-run, certain results. We might, for example, start a recession and perhaps before things pick up again we can find a good place to bury the idea until it is forgotten.

Even if the decision unit agrees to give the idea a trial, we have one more defense. If we can rig the feedback processes, we can still defeat this idea. We might arrange to have the wrong indicators used, or we might have appropriate indicators misinterpreted. Here I would enlist the help of those in the organization who feel they might be hurt if the idea is finally adopted; they may be able to throw some red herrings in front of the decision unit. If that doesn't work, perhaps we can arrange to have the feedback evaluated before the trial process is completed. If we can create at this point a crisis, such as recession, we may be able to abort the trial. If not, we might as well relax and enjoy it.

As a devil's advocate, I believe I see four levels for promoting the abortion of a good idea:

■ Personality level, by staffing the organization with deadheads.

■ Structural level, to prevent even "good personalities" from finding nourishment for an idea.

■ Administrative process, by interfering with decision-making, allocation, feedback, and evaluation.

■ Ecological, by creating environmental conditions and pressures which prevent good ideas from being adopted even under conditions of "good personalities," "good structure," and "good administrative process."

---

INNOVATION IN ORGANIZATION

*John T. Lanzetta*

---

To be useful to an organization, new solutions need not only to be created but accepted and implemented. I assume that:

■ Novel responses are more likely to be found in an active search. Serendipity occurs, but not very often.

■ Novel solutions are more likely to be accepted when they fit in with the overall strategies, preferences, and decision-making techniques of the organization.

People search for novel solutions when they have a problem and don't know how to solve it. The more important the problem, the stronger the motivation to search. But for the search to be continued, and to be reasonably likely to produce a novel alternative, it must be:

■ *Reinforced.* The organization must reward search and reduce the cost of acquiring information. The easier the access to consultants and experts, the greater the rewards for "idea men," the greater the likelihood that the search will be continued.

■ *Free of continuous evaluation.* Continuous evaluation can divert the search to a mere quest for data to bolster solutions already proposed, and may discourage other members of the organization from getting involved in the search.

■ *Free as possible of time limits.* Search tends to be curtailed when there are time pressures and, I suspect, is less efficient when faced with deadlines.

■ *Conducted by a large number of people of diverse training and background.* Informal problem solving should be wide-spread throughout the organization, rather than restricted to a formal planning section.

If a novel solution is clearly better than other solutions, it will most likely be accepted. But novel responses are difficult to evaluate; it is not always clear which alternative is "clearly better." In that case organizations tend to accept alternatives that fit in with their preferred ways of doing things.

An organization that prefers "high variance bets" is more likely to accept a novel alternative than one that prefers "low variance bets." Novel responses have a wide range of possible payoffs; they will lead either to a killing or to a heavy loss. An organization that commits its resources to such a venture is making a high variance bet. Organizations, like individuals, probably vary in their preference for high or low variance bets.

The outcome of a novel response is highly uncertain.

Organizations that have a greater tolerance for uncertainty are more likely to choose novel solutions.

Novel solutions, since they usually involve different ways of using resources, threaten vested interests in the organization. The parts of the organization that are threatened resist the acceptance of new ideas. Involvement in the search for new solutions seems to decrease this resistance, so that novel solutions are more likely to be chosen when very wide segments of the organization are committed to the search.

---

IGNORANCE, SUCCESS AND INNOVATION

*Harold J. Leavitt*

---

Ordinarily in organizations we associate creativity with a high degree of education—the scientist. But the scientist we are thinking about is the Ph.D. scientist, highly trained by other Ph.D. scientists, and working within some agreed-upon bounds—agreed upon not only by others in his own field, but by the whole world of Ph.D.'s in science. One wonders about the extent to which our shared educational processes, even at high levels, restrict search to those segments of the world accepted and prominently visible to the educated group.

We have recently come across an intriguing finding as a result of work on the common-target game. The common-target game is played with three or more participants, each blindfolded, each asked to hold up some number of fingers from zero to ten. The instructor calls out some whole number between zero and ten times the number of players. Each player is asked to hold up fingers such that the total of the whole group will add up to that target. Feedback of results can be varied, but usually the instructor says, "Your target was 25, you actually hit 23 with two eights and a seven." Subjects then try again for the target until they hit it; they are given a series of targets until they hit some criterion of proficiency.

Most of the subjects in our game have been undergraduate male students. Most of the time they organize rather effectively around a satisfactory and perfectly complete solution to the problem. But recently we have found that female fine arts and female high school students—although they usually organize much more sloppily, and are much less able to tell you what they are doing—are more likely to come up with a novel and probably better solution.

Most "analytically" trained subjects, like engineering students or mathematicians, tend to get organized quickly. They organize around a solution that involves the division of the target number by the number of subjects with sub-allocation of residuals among members. That is, if the target is 15, and there are three players, each takes five. If it's 16, two take 5 and one takes 6.

An alternative solution, which is simpler and more general, is seldom discovered by these players. This alternative solution involves the first man taking all whole targets up to and including 10, and then holding 10 beyond that. The second subject holds zeros until targets are over 10, and then takes anything within the second decile, and so on. This "peeling off" system, involving little arithmetic and fewer programmatic steps, seems to be discovered more frequently by women than men, and more frequently in situations where people are instructed to plan the game so that others can play it rather than to plan for themselves.

If one examines the process that the girls use that eventually leads them to discover the tens system, it tends to be essentially different from the direct, logical, divide-by-three solution used by boys. The boys generally start with an analysis of the task. They look at the target first, break it up into appropriate sized pieces, and then allocate the pieces to the persons. The stages in the process are these: (1) division of the target; (2) development of the scheme of allocation of residuals, and (3) assignment of persons to those residual roles.

The girls seem to operate in the opposite direction. They start by working out relationships with one another, with the target in a fuzzy, secondary, almost irrelevant role. They decide who will be group leader and who will respond to whom or adjust to whom. They ignore the target to concentrate on developing a local social system. If they miss the first time, they adjust to one another so they can hit the second time. Somehow, by a process I certainly don't understand, this activity eventually permits many of them to come up with this "peeling off by tens" solution.

We do not yet know why the girls behave this way. One hypothesis is that it is not because they are girls, but because they are mathematically undisciplined and ignorant. They are number-scared. They tend to look unhappy and make unpleasant cracks when they discover that they are in a numbers game. If this hypothesis is true, we would then have a situation where men, commonly trained and competent in dealing with numbers, take the prominent and commonly agreed upon path—immediate analysis of the target and division of it into parts. This apparently sensible direction of movement is also restrictive, limiting search to only one segment of the total range of possibilities. The girls, naive and number-ignorant, work on the relationships to one another and eventually end up searching the environment in areas not searched by the locked-step educated men.

___

CONDITIONS FOR INNOVATION

*Donald C. Pelz*

___

One growing conviction, supported by several bits of evidence, is that scientists don't create in a vacuum, but rise to the challenge of specific problems. Necessity, if not *the* mother of invention, is at least one of its progenitors. One effective function of the organization's leadership, therefore, can be to insure that scientists are brought face to face periodically with intriguing and important new problems.

One of our tentative findings so far is that scientists having high autonomy are not necessarily the most productive. Rather, the optimal condition seems to be one in which the scientist has considerable *influence* on the direction of his own technical work, but at the same time exposes himself to the ideas of *several other decision-makers* concerning choice of his technical goals (such as colleagues, immediate chief, higher executive levels, or outside clients or sponsors).

Confronting the scientist with problems is not done by fiat or arbitrary assignment. A number of better mechanisms are available—a problem-oriented bull session, off-the-record conferences, small meetings involving (a) the scientist himself, (b) his immediate supervisor, (c) a potential user of the research such as a manufacturing or sales official who has a problem, (d) three or four colleagues with relevant skills.

One theory considers creativity to consist essentially of taking elements from unrelated areas and combining them in useful new ways. If this is the case, creativity is likely to rise in proportion to the range or scope of areas which are scanned for possible new elements.

One of the persistent trends in our data is that scientific output rises in proportion to several measures of diversity in the individual's working tasks.

■ Scientists who report a specialized knowledge of three or four specific areas are more productive than those with specialized knowledge in one or two areas.

■ Those who concentrate in a single kind of R & D—basic research, applied research, product improvement, product invention, technical services—are less effective than those who spend at least some time on several of these areas.

■ Scientists who put 100 percent of their time on their technical work (research or development) are less effective than those who put a quarter or a third time on administration or communication.

■ Groups which develop narrow specialties lose their effectiveness after a few years, while groups which maintain an interest in pioneering maintain their vitality.

Management can see to it that individuals and groups are prodded to move into additional areas by deliberately tossing a problem to a unit that is *not* most practiced in handling that type of problem.

While management can help to confront the scientist with important problems and stimulate diversity of information input, it remains for the scientist to get thoroughly absorbed by his problems if innovation is to occur. Maximum scientific output (and I am inclined to think maximum innovation, also) occurs in the presence of two somewhat contradictory elements: internally-based commitment or excitement about a problem area, and exposure to external inputs. Sheer isolation, while it may maximize internal commitment, is not a fruitful condition for a high rate of either scientific output or innovation.

How can internalized commitment—call it "curiosity" if you wish—be enhanced without cutting off communication? While the individual defends his ideas periodically before colleagues or superiors, he nevertheless has considerable voice in the final decision as to what he does. Research teams must be small; decisions about funds and resources must be relatively decentralized, so that the individual—or a relatively small set of colleagues—retains substantial control over the means to carry out his objectives. His requests must not be subject to veto by layers of review committees.

There is some evidence that scientific output is enhanced by intellectual competition, either among individuals or among groups. Scientific competition in its worse forms can be deadly, but in mild forms invigorating.

A scientific organization, therefore, must be large enough so that each individual has two or three colleagues in a similar field and of similar status with whom he can feel friendly competition. The organization should have sufficient members in proportion to diversity of technical skills, so that each man is not an unchallenged expert.

The social structure should be relatively unstratified. If each man knows exactly where he stands on the prestige ladder, competition between individuals is minimized. Status ambiguity can be enhanced by periodic organizational reshuffling, so that no one feels he has a permanent superior or a permanent set of subordinates. The most brilliant member of a group should not be its supervisor. Otherwise his organizational status reinforces his intellectual status. "Division of labor" among research groups sounds reasonable for assembly line productivity, but can impede innovation. Two or more groups competing to solve the same problem—perhaps by different routes—can stimulate each other's creativity.

My highly speculative hunch is that as the scientist matures, his psychological time mechanism runs slower. One year in college at age 20 seems ample to explore whole disciplines; one year on a research project at age 40 seems barely time to get the project under way. Perhaps this phenomenon results from a well-known psychophysical rule: the larger a stimulus, the larger must be an increment to produce a "just noticeable difference." Relative to the time that has gone before, each succeeding year becomes proportionately smaller.

Our data indicate a phenomenon that may be related. As research groups stay together beyond four or five years, they become successively less productive. This process is accompanied by a general slowing down in the group process; a drop in the rate of communication with colleagues, a drop in the feeling of competition among individuals or between groups. The data also suggest that old groups which continue to behave like young groups—which maintain a high rate of interaction, a high degree of individual or particularly of group competition—also continue to be effective.

I suspect further that the passage of time on scientific projects is geared to an information cycle. The scientist asks a question, seeks information to answer the question, inspects the data in order to formulate a new question, and so on. The rate at which this question-answer-question cycle repeats itself is critical, I think, to the subjective passage of research time. And I suspect that as individuals or groups age, the cycle slows down.

Management can perhaps do three kinds of things to keep research time from slowing down excessively. One is to see that periodic opportunities for review are scheduled

—seminars for progress reports, conferences among people working in similar areas, publication of articles or books. The presence of these "benign deadlines" gives structure to time.

Management can help to see that delays in the question asking and answering process are kept to a minimum. The supporting services needed for data collection or data reduction should be closely watched to prevent delays.

Management can encourage scientists to start a new project before the last drop is milked from the old one, or to join an exciting new group to work on an intriguing new problem, even though the old group has not completely exhausted the old problem. Starting afresh always speeds up the time clock, and so does the approach of some deadline or termination point.

---

ORGANIZATION-CREATING ORGANIZATIONS

*Arthur Stinchcombe*

---

Some organizations seem to sprout new organizations at a great rate, and others hardly ever give rise to new organizations. Some outstanding cases of organization-creating organizations are the Teamsters' Union in the United States, the *Partido Revolutionario Institutional* in Mexico, the Communist parties when they have come to power in Eastern Europe and Asia, several great corporations such as AT&T, General Motors, General Electric, and Lever Brothers, the CIO organizing committee in the 1930's, some of the mercantilist states of early modern times (creating among other things the corporations which eventually became new nations), and at various times the Roman church.

On the other hand, it has historically been fairly rare,

I think, for armies, many banks and insurance companies, or colleges and universities until fairly recent times to sprout in this fashion.

When we speak of "entrepreneurship" we generally have had an image of what an entrepreneur looks like—a man grubbing along until he gets rich enough to hire some trusty lieutenants to grub along with him, getting over obstacles by luck and pluck rather than by the use of resources already concentrated for that purpose, perhaps recruited from some underprivileged group and with high achievement motivation. The setting up of the Edsel Division, or of the Communist trade unions in the Soviet Union after the revolution, or of peanut cultivation in East Africa, or of warehouse unions under the Teamsters, was not much like that. We need not go as far as Marx and call the "luck and pluck" theory "the myth of primitive accumulation" in order to realize that organizations are sometimes more than the lengthened shadow of a man.

It seems to me that three things are crucial for such organization-creating organizations.

■ In the first place, in most of these cases there has been a relatively large fund of resources (political legitimacy, money, force, ideological commitment of an inner core) which had been received from the society (either by historical accident or by credit from past achievement) without tieing the hands of the elite which controlled it. For instance, the official party of Mexico got its political power granted on the general basis of a nationalistic and revolutionary ideology, rather than specific limited power for particular purposes. Similarly, a blue-chip company need not justify an offering of stocks by a specific promise that the money will be used for a particular purpose (as a uranium mining company implicitly has to) but on the basis of its general credit and past record. This leaves the blue-chip company (but not the uranium mining company) free to use the resources to develop new sets of roles integrated around new purposes.

■ Besides the concentration of resources on the basis of general trust or generalized values, it is crucial that the organization be capable of "creative destruction" within the organization for it to sprout new organizations. Organizations differ in the degree of vesting of interests within the organization. In universities, for instance, generalized resources recruited by the organization are rapidly fixed into commitments to specialized subunits. They might as well have been fixed to a specific purpose to start with, as far as their usefulness for creating new organizations within the university is concerned. It happens that in this case the vesting of interests preserves different kinds of values of innovation (innovation by individuals in the basic intellectual disciplines), which I happen to be in favor of, but the organizational point remains. Universities cannot use resources which are committed to them on the basis of their general reputation very easily to set up new organizations of any type, because the collegial control system and the tenure system result in the rapid vesting of interests in bits and pieces of the general university budget.

Organizations that are in some respects internally tyrannical, in which subordinates do not have easily defensible vested interests, can destroy a subunit if necessary either to stamp out opposition or to free resources to move in an apparently more profitable direction. In the Mexican PRI, the Presidents (especially Calles and Cardenas) had enough legitimacy as individual heroes of the revolution to destroy the independent power of regional *caudillos* and the army generals. They were able to carry through successfully what Perón in Argentina failed to do, to create new interest group organizations which would support the party and give it freedom of action by making it less dependent on the army. Once this was accomplished the party could continue to innovate by creating a new set of organizations to represent other interest groups (especially professionals and petty bourgeoisie) and build them into the Party apparatus. The point is that the "tyranny" of the Presidents of Mexico within the PRI favored the destruction of the power of one vested interest (that of the army) and hence allowed the development of other organizations.

The relatively high degree of freedom to fire or transfer people held by business organizations in the United States (but not everywhere) has the same importance. If the Edsel division had been a new department in a university, it would still be there. And it would prevent new adventures by tying up resources and by opposing the diversion of energies into new lines.

■ A third factor that I think is important is the degree of organization of the "market" for organizational services. This is, of course, a characteristic of the environment of the organization rather than of the organization itself. Consider the difference between an *organized market* and a *mass market*. In order to find out exactly what is wanted in an organized market, one need only ask the organized customers' leaders what they want. These leaders will have already aggregated the needs of the market (saving economists considerable trouble) since they have intimate acquaintance with the needs and since the petition-making process from the market will focus on them. And consider also the behavior of the market over time during the period of innovation, in making the jump from no consumption to substantial consumption. This jump can be a jump in an organized market, so that the market goes suddenly from taking none of the "product" to taking quite a lot of it, while in a "mass" market the sales will increase as more of the product appears, gradually adding one little customer after another. What these two factors mean is that the organized market will more often yield the degree of certainty and "lumpiness" to justify meek men in organizational roles committing a large bunch of resources to a new purpose. In a mass market, on the contrary, the uncertainty and the slow growth usually to be expected make it both easier and more rational to build up the business from scratch. Thus "entrepreneurship" in the classical sense is likely in a "mass" market, while an organized market is likely to give rise to new entrepreneurship in already existing organizations.

---

THE INNOVATING METROPOLIS

*Richard L. Meier*

---

Cities can specialize in fundamental research, applied research and invention, development, in the exploitation of such creative efforts (innovation), or in a combination of these.

Such specialization has hitherto been an accident of history, with no general goal or plan set up in advance. Henceforth attempts will be made to *plan* cities so that they innovate. It will be done by consciously fostering research and development, and assisting the firms and professional groups that are created to utilize new knowledge. The city will prosper because some of the innovations are likely to succeed, and the wealth that is created will accumulate in the city as the "home plant" expands its employment and the "home office" subsidizes back-up services.

Forced-draft technical innovation today, in most fields outside of medicine, is best carried out in the urban region of Southern California. Most government departments and large corporations have come to recognize the potentials of the Los Angeles area and have either had to establish permanent links with one or more organizations there or buy up a smaller enterprise and develop it as a subsidiary. The *quality* of the research and development is not extraordinary as compared to the rest of the country, but the flexibility and speed in assembling an organization capable of tackling a given technical problem is unparalleled. Why is this so and how does it come about?

The foremost consideration has been the scarcity of engineers, physicists, applied mathematicians, computer programmers, and related technicians. Research entrepreneurs who wish to build an organization depend heavily upon "psychic income" as an attraction, even more than upon pay scale. The high educational level, the opportunity to live in new communities suited to one's taste, the youth and informality, superimposed upon solid technical achievements in the aviation industry have made Southern California exceedingly attractive to a college-educated post-war generation whose origins were in the Middle West and South. Many Easterners were attracted by the cosmopolitan culture and year-round gardening. The immigrants came despite the fact that job security was relatively poor; all of them were gambling their careers on a rising research market.

The striking fact in Southern California is mobility. Technical people seem to change organizations every two or three years while elsewhere they make two or three changes in a lifetime. The organizations themselves have fat years and thin years, depending upon their luck with research and development contracts. One sees, therefore, a population of perhaps 100,000 professionals and top technicians grouping and re-grouping to process practical problems that are up for bid, mainly from Washington. Only a city based upon automobile transportation could combine the preferred living patterns of research personnel with the organizational mobility needed for processing the complex crash programs from the Pentagon and the National Aeronautics and Space Agency. Research engineers in the West Los Angeles and San Diego areas are always confident that jobs will be opening up within commuting distance as the present contract draws to an end. They would not be forced to pick up the family and move to a more convenient location. Urban form on the Peninsula is also automobile-oriented, but the region seems to maintain, in research as well as taste, a sophistication that is a notch or so higher than Southern California. This is due largely to the attempts of Stanford University to capture for itself some of the external economies associated with research-oriented universities.

The Stanford story is a classic example of the discovery and exploitation of hidden opportunities created by the growth of research-oriented technology. A land-rich, but endowment-poor, private university first started a research unit, the Stanford Research Institute, which quickly became the largest of the nonprofit applied research organizations in the country. By being alert to opportunities all over the world, catholic in its research interests, and able to draw upon repositories of knowledge, particularly libraries and skill, that had been patiently accumulated in a university community for decades, it broke down a long standing compartmentation of effort and provided bases for growth in new directions, particularly business research and broad gauge technical assistance overseas. The tract of land that had been reached by the growing fringe of the San Francisco metropolitan complex would inevitably have generated some significant values, but a sizable multiplier was obtained due to the presence of the faculty, the library, and alumni loyalty.

Boston, with its Route 128, has a comparable development although on a still larger scale. Here it was a notable combination between a technical entrepreneurial tradition maintained at the Massachusetts Institute of Technology, which respected a man even more highly if he went into business on the side and developed his own discoveries in the form of salable components, and a long tradition in investment banking that was not satisfied with run-of-the-mill propositions. The amenities of the outer suburbs made it possible to attract technical personnel (particularly from California!) and the location of the Route made it possible to assemble a sub-professional labor force from the youngsters leaving the declining mill towns. Here, too, it was possible to build up a critical mass of professional personnel, but further growth is greatly hampered by the inability in the Boston area for the technicians to go to night school and work their way into professional status. Boston is the only major metropolitan area where a break exists in the technical training programs that requires taking leave from the job or quitting.

This planning has been piecemeal, and agencies in charge of metropolitan development have created projects without careful calculation of cultural interactions. The task appears to be that of assigning locations to new activities so that the information about technical capabilities encounters information about uses in application earlier, and with greater persuasiveness, than in competing metropolitan areas. Academic research should be good, the people anxious to apply it should be close at hand, and the others that understand finance and markets should be almost as accessible. Matchmakers should be allowed to move through all these groups without encountering social barriers.

A partial set of rules most likely to lead to success may be outlined:

■ Maintain an open society for scientists, technologists, managers, and associated specialists who work with innovating entrepreneurs.

■ Encourage the utmost variety in living styles available to such individuals (currently music, fine arts, drama, fine foods, skiing, sailing, skin-diving, and flying should be emphasized to reinforce typical styles of innovators).

■ Provide homesites with maximum differentiation, from urbane apartment blocks to pieces of wilderness.

■ Build new light industrial and office structures around an established research-oriented university or hospital, or a stock of basic knowledge—such as a good library.

■ Locate near the best technically trained sub-professionals (usually working in heavy industry) so that they can contact the growing technical installations and can be recruited as desired.

■ Maximize accessibility (via expressway and communications systems) to downtown center, international airport, and the wilderness areas (sea and mountain).

■ Sponsor designs for buildings that are neither elitist nor lowbrow, but range between utilitarian and avant garde.

■ Build up the quality of the secondary schools, both public and private.

■ Stimulate some interaction independent of employment,

profession, and principal cultural interest (PTA, neighborhood block group, cooperative nursery schools, voluntary civic group) to build up a steady diffusion of ideas through informal channels.

This form of social planning is still rare, but some rather sophisticated examples can be cited. Many of the techniques for implementation have yet to be formulated. The object is to build an adaptive system which metabolizes *information* as rapidly, and with as small an error frequency, as the best that has evolved. For the time being the greatest volume of such information is scientific and technical, so most of the innovating metropoles must be biased in that direction, but there may be room for a few such as Washington which process political and cultural data predominantly.

---

## NECESSITY VERSUS THE DEVIL

*James Q. Wilson*

---

The behavioral theory of the firm confronts the student with two theories of innovation, each most simply stated as a proverb: "Necessity is the mother of invention," and "The devil makes work for idle hands."

The proverbs really describe the working of two kinds of innovative processes. One is "problem-solving" and is the result of declining performance. The organization looks about for a way out of its difficulty. Proposed changes are measured against organizational goals and must seem profitable in the short term. An atmosphere of crisis prevails. Organizational resources are in short supply; requests by subunits for shares of these resources are evaluated stringently; to conserve resources, economies are instituted. Cost-cutting is a common problem-solving innovation. When a new process is adopted, it is because it will permit a cut-back in more costly production factors—such as employees. Necessity is the mother of invention.

Other organizations, more blessed by fortune, have rising performance levels. The original goals are perhaps out-stripped. An atmosphere of success pervades the firm. Resources are accumulated in excess of those required to maintain the organization; as a result, subunit demands for shares of those resources are treated generously. New ideas need not be justified in the short run nor closely related to immediate organizational goals. Not much attention is paid to costs and imaginations are free to "plan ahead" for a vaguely-perceived tomorrow. New products and processes are conceived and sometimes adopted, not because they are immediately needed but because some member or subunit has sufficient excess resources (time, energy, manpower) to devote to bright ideas. The devil makes work for idle hands.

The devil theory of innovation was devised, as I understand it, because the necessity theory was not supported by the facts. Being on the ragged edge of adversity did not appear to make firms more inventive or more adaptive; on the contrary, the prosperous firms seemed more willing to try new ideas. A theory was obviously necessary to show why successful firms innovated; if this could be done without abandoning the previous theory—that unsuccessful firms innovated also, but in a different way—so much the better. Necessity and the devil could be brought into a fruitful partnership.

The distinction between what I call necessity and the devil is at least a good beginning. As a political scientist, it has for me the appeal of drawing attention to the existence in organizations of two different kinds of processes that are to be found also in governments and societies. In political analysis we speak of the "politics of scarcity" and the "politics of abundance." Necessity—scarcity-induced change—is of course characteristic of many of the newer, recently independent nations, whereas the devil—the politics of abundance and affluence—is found in certain advanced nations. Some propositions have been devised about these two kinds of political systems which may be applicable to formal organizations:

■ In a political system characterized by scarcity, law is more repressive than restitutive; illegality is an offense against the collectivity and must be treated as an act of disloyalty rather than an infraction of a rule.

■ In a politics of scarcity, law and custom tend to be complementary and even indistinguishable; in a politics of abundance, custom is often at variance with law and serves to protect individuals and groups from law.

■ In a politics of abundance, conflict is moderated by increasing the resources of all competing groups (relying on growth or unused resources to make the payments) ; in a politics of scarcity, conflict is met by redistributing existing resources or by suppression.

■ Scarcity is associated with centralization, abundance with decentralization. If resources are few, their allocation must be made centrally in order to achieve economies of scale, to insure that only approved goals are served, and to prevent frictional losses. Abundance permits social choice to replace central decision-making.

■ In a centralized system of scarcity, the desire for change in a subunit often requires paying (e.g., bribing) the central agency in order to obtain the necessary freedom of action; in a decentralized system of abundance, the desire for change in the system as a whole often requires bribing subunits in order to obtain the necessary consent. Since centralized scarcity implies that there will be relatively few "free" resources adrift in the system, it will be very difficult to obtain consent for localized innovation except (rarely) by persuasion. Since decentralized abundance implies a very great distribution of sizable free resources, it will be very costly to concert the wills of enough subunits to permit system-wide innovation.

I think there are some easy (perhaps too easy) analogies here between nations and organizations. Certain firms in the grip of a politics of scarcity—railroads or coal mines, for example—are engaged in suppressing conflict, maintaining (or trying to reassert) hierarchical controls, eliminating unproductive elements, resisting bargaining, and proclaiming the supremacy of certain explicit organizational goals (such as profit). Other firms, luxuriating in a rising market, are more likely to be avoiding conflict, relaxing hierarchical controls, encouraging bargaining, proliferating new products and processes, and engaging in the prolix elaboration of fuzzy, statesman-like "goals." We often call the necessitous firms "backward" and the devilish firms "progressive" and "innovative." This either indicates a narrow use of the term "innovation" or a social science preference for the devil.

---

## CURIOSITY AND OPPORTUNISM

*John C. Wright*

---

I would like to distinguish two quite different patterns of problem solving. One I shall call intuitive opportunism, and the other systematic curiosity. As the name implies, intuitive opportunism is characterized by goal-oriented guessing. Usually there is no clear organization of the logical possibilities and no systematic plan for testing alternatives or keeping track of where one is in the strategic search sequence. Failure has little impact; it acts simply as a signal to keep searching. In deliberately ambiguous experimental situations we have found that this pattern predominates both when success is very frequent and very easily achieved, and when information storage and retrieval (the memory and bookkeeping systems) are inadequately organized or overloaded. The pattern tends to occur whenever search activity is made more important than search strategy, and results more important than either. Like brainstorming sessions, such searches produce a great quantity of variable responses, most of which would be immediately discarded if they were evaluated carefully on the basis of what is already known.

Systematic curiosity patterns involve a determination to exhaust the array of possibilities rather than to settle for a good solution in hand. Usually tests that have failed in the past are not repeated, but alternatives that have worked successfully in the past are similarly discarded on the grounds that there exist others that have not yet been tried. This kind of compulsive novelty seeking tends to occur in situations where success has had insufficient impact and distinctiveness, and where the outlook for finding a satisfactory solution is most pessimistic. The reinforcement for such patterns comes from the acquisition of new information more than from the achievement of a solution. Individuals employing this pattern never make the same mistake twice, but often fail to see the advantages of partial successes achieved until the systematic search plan has been exhausted. They seem to be motivated by disciplined curiosity rather than by opportunism.

Although intuitive opportunism thrives on the nurturant environment we try to provide for applied creativity (non-critical, openminded, anything goes), it is often focussed so much on the immediate goal or solution that promising detours not strictly relevant to the main program are often ignored and lost. What is more, these search patterns are inefficient in that they are not cumulative. The record left by such a search resembles the shambles left in my study when the children have been turned loose there on an Easter egg hunt.

The rigors of systematic curiosity, on the other hand, insure not only that search produces a cumulative record useful in preventing repetitive errors, but also that the searcher himself has an organized plan of attack and knows where he is going and where he has been. One advantage is that he can learn from failure where the intuitive oppor-tunist cannot. Search organized on the basis of systematic curiosity thrives on adversity, at least in the sense that it is specifically designed to make steady progress by rejecting negative alternatives. Like an air-rescue team searching for a downed flyer, its efficiency is based on a plan of carefully scanning and checking off miles of empty ocean, a process which itself maintains or even increases vigilance for any exception to the monotonous chain of negative results.

If both of these patterns have weaknesses, they are also both capable of producing successful innovation. It is un-likely that either pattern alone has as much capacity for producing effective innovation as a proper combination of the two would have. Such an optimal combination will most certainly depend upon the nature of the task.

One possible criterion for determining which kind of search pattern to encourage is this: If the range of possible solutions seems broad, uncertain, and disorganized, more progress is likely to result from systematic, curiosity oriented search. Conversely, if the range is narrow, well organized and familiar, then intuitive opportunism might prove to be more effective. Imagine yourself a rather poor golfer who has just hit a wicked slice off the third tee and into the rough. The problem is to find the ball. If your slice is an old familiar curse with fairly constant and predictable angle and distance, if you know the course well and are painfully familiar with a couple of low spots 150 yards down the right-hand rough, if you saw the ball vanish near some readily identifiable landmarks, and if you have a past record of good luck in finding lost balls, your best bet is to play your hunches and look where your best guess tells you the ball has landed. Your second best hunch should tell you where to look next, etc.

If, on the other hand, your slice is a random thing, if you are unfamiliar with the course, if you did not get a good look at the flight of the ball, and if your intuitive hunches have tended to be wrong in the past, then your best strategy is to comb the area back and forth in three-foot swaths, just as you mow your lawn. Though it is slow and may appear unimaginative, the systematic pattern will surely find the ball if it is there. And unlike the good guesser, the systematic searcher is likely to find not only his own ball, but several others and perhaps a diamond earring as well!

May it not be that serendipity favors the genuinely curious over the cleverly opportunistic?

*January/February 1965*

# Post Bureaucratic Leadership

WARREN G. BENNIS

In an early issue of this magazine (*Trans*-action, June-July 1965), I forecast that in the next 25 to 50 years we would participate in the end of bureaucracy as we know it and in the rise of new social systems better suited to the 20th century demands of industrialization. The prediction was based on the evolutionary principle that every age develops an organizational form appropriate to its genius, and that the prevailing form today—the pyramidal, centralized, functionally specialized, impersonal mechanism known as *bureaucracy*—was out of joint with contemporary realities.

This breakdown of a venerable form of organization so appropriate to 19th century conditions is caused, I argued, by a number of factors, but chiefly the following four: 1) rapid and unexpected change; 2) growth in size beyond what is necessary for the work being done (for example, inflation caused by bureaucratic overhead and tight

165

controls, impersonality caused by sprawls, outmoded rules, and organizational rigidities) ; 3) complexity of modern technology, in which integration between activities and persons of very diverse, highly specialized competence is required; 4) a change in managerial values toward more humanistic democratic practices.

Organizations of the future, I predicted, will have some unique characteristics. They will be adaptive, rapidly changing *temporary systems,* organized around problems-to-be-solved by groups of relative strangers with diverse professional skills. The groups will be arranged on organic rather than mechanical models; they will evolve in response to problems rather than to programmed expectations. People will be evaluated, not in a rigid vertical hierarchy according to rank and status, but flexibly, according to competence. Organizational charts will consist of project groups rather than stratified functional groups, as is now the case. Adaptive, problem-solving, temporary systems of diverse specialists, linked together by coordinating executives in an organic flux—this is the organizational form that will gradually replace bureaucracy.

Ironically, the bold future I had predicted is now routine and can be observed wherever the most interesting and advanced practices exist. Most of these trends are visible and have been surfacing for years in the aerospace, construction, drug, and consulting industries as well as professional and research and development organizations, which only shows that the distant future now has a way of arriving before the forecast is fully comprehended.

A question left unanswered, however, has to do with leadership. How would these new organizations be managed? Are there any transferable lessons from present managerial practices? Do the behavioral sciences provide any suggestions? How can these complex, ever-changing, free-form, kaleidoscopic patterns be coordinated? Of course there can be no definitive answers, but unless we can understand the leadership requirements for organizations of the future, we shall inevitably back blindly into it rather than cope with it effectively.

Accepted theory and conventional wisdom concerning leadership have a lot in common. Both seem to be saying that the success of a leader depends on the leader, the led, and the unique situation. This formulation—abstract and majestically useless—is the best that can be gleaned from over 100 years of research on "leadership."

On the other hand, any formulations may be inadequate and pallid compared to the myths and primitive psychological responses that surround such complexities as leadership and power. Our preoccupation with the mystiques of the Kennedys is sufficient reminder of that.

Thus, leadership theory coexists with a powerful and parallel archetypal reality. But in what follows, we shall see that it is the latter myth that is threatened—the aggressive, inner-directed 19th century autocrat. For the moment, though, I want to quickly review some of the key situational features likely to confront the leader of the future.

The overarching feature is change itself, its accelerating rate and its power to transform. The phrase "the only constant is change" has reached the point of a cliché, which at once anesthetizes us to its pain and stimulates grotesque fantasies about a Brave New World with no place in the sun for us. Change is the "godhead" term for our age as it has not been for any other. One has only to recall that the British Parliament was debating in the last part of the 19th century whether to close up the Royal

Patent Office, as it was felt that all significant inventions had already been discovered.

But what are the most salient changes affecting human organization, the ones with most relevance to their governance? Foremost is the changing nature of our institutions. In 1947, employment stood at approximately 58 million and now is at about 72 million. According to V. K. Fuchs, "Virtually all of this increase occurred in industries that provide services, for example, banks, hospitals, retail stores, and schools." This nation has become the only country to employ more people in services than in production of tangible goods. The growth industries today, if we can call them that, are education, health, welfare, and other professional institutions. The problem facing organizations is no longer manufacturing—it is the management of large-scale sociotechnical systems and the strategic deployment of high-grade professional talent.

There are other important correlates and consequences of change. For example, the working population will be younger, smarter, and more mobile. Half of our country's population is under 25, and one out of every three persons is 15 years of age or younger. More people are going to college; over half go to college in certain urban areas. The United States Postal Department reports that one out of every five families changes its address every year.

Most of these changes compel us to look beyond bureaucracy for newer models of organizations that have the capability to cope with contemporary conditions. The general direction of these changes—toward more service and professional organizations, toward more educated, younger, and mobile employees, toward more diverse, complex, science-based systems, toward a more turbulent and uncertain environment—forces us to consider new styles of leadership. Leading the enterprise of the future becomes a significant social process, requiring as much, if not more, managerial than substantive competence. Robert McNamara is a case in point. Before he came to Washington, he was considered for three Cabinet positions: Defense, State, and Treasury. His "only" recommendation was that he was a superior administrator. Chris Argyris has concluded that success or failure in the United States Department of State depends as much or more on one's interpersonal and managerial competence as one's substantive knowledge of "diplomacy." It can also be said that leadership of modern organizations depends on new forms of knowledge and skills not necessarily related to the primary task of the organization. In short, the pivotal function in the leader's role has changed away from a sole concern with the substantive to an emphasis on the interpersonal and organizational processes.

One convenient focus for a discussion of leadership is to review the main problems confronting modern organizations, and to understand the kinds of tasks and strategies linked to the solution of these problems.

## Contributions and Inducements

A simple way to understand this problem is to compute the ratio between what an individual gives and what he gets in his day-to-day transactions. In other words, are the contributions to the organization about equivalent to the inducements received? Where there is a high ratio between inducements and contributions, either the organization or the employee gets restless and searches for different environments, or different people.

There is nothing startling or new about this formulation. Nevertheless, organizations frequently do not know what is truly rewarding, especially for the professionals and highly trained workers who will dominate the organizations of the future. With this class of employee, conventional policies and practices regarding incentives, never particularly sensitive, tend to be inapplicable.

Most organizations regard economic rewards as the primary incentive to peak performance. These are not unimportant to the professional, but, if economic rewards are equitable, other incentives become far more potent. Avarice, to paraphrase Hume, is *not* the spirit of industry, particularly of professionals. Professionals tend to seek such rewards as full utilization of their talent and training; professional status (not necessarily within the organization, but externally with respect to their profession); and opportunities for development and further learning. The main difference between the professional and the more conventional, hourly employee is that the former will not yield "career authority" to the organization.

The most important incentive, then, is to "make it" professionally, to be respected by professional colleagues. Loyalty to an organization may increase if it encourages professional growth. (I was told recently that a firm decided to build all future plants in university towns in order to attract and hold on to college-trained specialists.) The "good place to work" resembles a super-graduate school, alive with dialogue and senior colleagues, where the employee will not only work to satisfy organizational demands, but, perhaps primarily, those of his profession.

The other incentive is self-realization, personal growth that may not be task-related. I'm well aware that that remark questions four centuries of an encrusted Protestant ethic, reinforced by the indispensability of work for the preservation and justification of existence. But work, as we all must experience it, serves at least two psychic functions: first, that of binding man more closely to reality; and secondly, in Freud's terms, "of displacing a large amount of libidinal components, whether narcissistic, aggressive, or even erotic, onto professional work and onto human relations connected with it . . ."

It is not at all clear as to how, or even if, these latter needs can be deliberately controlled by the leadership. Company-sponsored courses, sensitivity training sessions, and other so-called adult education courses may, in fact, reflect these needs. Certainly attitudes toward "continuing education" are changing. The idea that education has a terminal point and that college students come in only 4 sizes—18, 19, 20, and 21—is old-fashioned. A "dropout" should be redefined to mean anyone who hasn't *returned* to school.

Whichever way the problem of professional and personal growth is resolved, it is clear that many of the older forms of incentives, based on the more elementary needs (safety-economic-physiological) will have to be reconstituted. Even more profound will be the blurring of the boundaries between work and play, between the necessity to belong and the necessity to achieve, which 19th century mores have unsuccessfully attempted to compartmentalize.

*The Problem of Distributing Power*

There are many issues involved in the distribution of power: psychological, practical, and moral. I will consider only the practical side, with obvious implications for the other two. To begin with, it is quaint to think that one man, no matter how omniscient and omnipotent, can comprehend, let alone control, the diversity and complexity of the modern organization. Followers and leaders who think this is possible get trapped in a child's fantasy of absolute power and absolute dependence.

Today it is hard to realize that during the Civil War, "government" (Lincoln's executive staff) had fewer than 50 civilian subordinates, and not many executives at that, chiefly telegraph clerks and secretaries. Even so recent an administration as Franklin Roosevelt's had a cozy, "family" tone about it. According to his doctor, for example, Roosevelt "loved to know everything that was going on and delighted to have a finger in every pie."

"Having a finger in every pie" may well be an occupational disease of presidents, but it is fast becoming outmoded. Today's administration must reflect the necessities imposed by size and complexity. In fact, there has been a general tendency to move tacitly away from a "presidential" form of power to a "cabinet" or team concept, with some exceptions (like Union Carbide) where "team management" has been conceptualized and made explicit. There is still a long-standing pseudomasculine tendency to disparage such plural executive arrangements, but they are on the increase.

This system of an "executive constellation" by no means implies an abdication of responsibility by the chief executive. It should reflect a coordinated effort based on the distinct competencies of the individual. It is a way of multiplying executive power through a realistic allocation of effort. Of course, this means also that top executive personnel are chosen not only on the basis of their unique talents but on how these skills and competencies fit and work together.

Despite all the problems inherent in the executive constellation concept—how to build an effective team, compatibility, etc.—it is hard to see other valid ways to handle the sheer size and overload of the leader's role.

*The Control of Conflict*

Related to the problem of developing an effective executive constellation is another key task of the leader—building a climate in which collaboration, not conflict, will flourish. An effective, collaborative climate is easier to experience and harder to achieve than a formal description of it, but most students of group behavior would agree that it should include the following ingredients: flexible and adaptive structure, utilization of individual talents, clear and agreed-upon goals, standards of openness, trust, and cooperation, interdependence, high intrinsic rewards, and transactional controls—which means a lot of individual autonomy, and a lot of participation making key decisions.

Developing this group "synergy" is difficult, and most organizations take the easy way out—a "zero-synergy" strategy. This means that the organization operates under the illusion that they can hire the best individuals in the world, and then adopt a Voltairean stance of allowing each to cultivate his own garden. This strategy of isolation can best be observed in universities, where it operates with great sophistication. The Berkeley riots were symptomatic of at least four self-contained, uncommunicating social systems (students, faculty, administration, regents) without the trust, empathy and interaction—to say nothing of the tradition—to develop meaningful collaboration. To make matters worse, academics by nature, reinforced by tradition, see themselves as "loners." They want to be independent together, so to speak. Academic narcissism goes a long way on the lecture platform, but may be positively dysfunctional for developing a community.

Another equally pernicious strategy with the same effects, but different style (and more typical of American business institutions), is a pseudodemocratic "groupiness" characterized by false harmony and avoidance of conflict.

Synergy is hard to develop. Lack of experience and strong cultural biases against group efforts worsen the problem. Groups, like other highly complicated organisms, need time to develop. They need a gestation period to develop interaction, trust, communication, and commitment. No one should expect an easy maturity in groups any more than in young children.

Expensive and time-consuming as it is, building synergetic and collaborative cultures will become essential. Modern problems are too complex and diversified for one man or one discipline. They require a blending of skills and perspectives, and only effective problem-solving units will be able to master them.

*Responding to a Turbulent, Uncertain Environment*

In the early days of the last war when armaments of all kinds were in short supply, the British, I am told, made use of a venerable field piece that had come down to them from previous generations. The honorable past of this light artillery stretched back, in fact, to the Boer War. In the days of uncertainty after the fall of France, these guns, hitched to trucks, served as useful mobile units in the coast defense. But it was felt that the rapidity of fire could be increased. A time-motion expert was, therefore, called into suggest ways to simplify the firing procedures. He watched one of the gun crews of five men at practice in the field for some time. Puzzled by certain aspects of the procedures, he took some slow-motion pictures of the soldiers performing the loading, aiming, and firing routines.

When he ran those pictures over once or twice, he

noticed something that appeared odd to him. A moment before the firing, two members of the gun crew ceased all activity and came to attention for a three-second interval extending throughout the discharge of the gun. He summoned an old colonel of artillery, showed him the pictures, and pointed out this strange behavior. What, he asked the colonel, did it mean? The colonel, too, was puzzled. He asked to see the pictures again. "Ah," he said when the performance was over, "'I have it. They are holding the horses." (Elting Morison, *Man, Machines and Modern Times*, 1966)

This fable demonstrates nicely the pain with which man accommodates to change. And yet, characteristically and ironically, he continues to seek out new inventions which disorder his serenity and undermine his competence.

One striking index of the rapidity of change—for me, the single, most dramatic index—is the shrinking interval between the time of a discovery and its commercial application. Before World War I, the lag between invention and utilization was 33 years, between World War I and World War II, it was 17 years. After World War II, the interval decreased to about nine years, and if the future can be extrapolated on the basis of the past, by 1970 it will be around five to six years. The transistor was discovered in 1948, and by 1960, 95 percent of all the important equipment and over 50 percent of *all* electronic equipment utilized them in place of conventional vacuum tubes. The first industrial application of computers was as recent as 1956.

Modern organizations, even more than individuals, are acutely vulnerable to the problem of responding flexibly and appropriately to new information. Symptoms of maladaptive responses, at the extremes, are a guarded, frozen, rigidity that denies the presence or avoids the recognition of changes that will result most typically in organizational paralysis; or, at the opposite extreme, an overly receptive, susceptible gullibility to change resulting in a spastic, unreliable faddism. It is obvious that there are times when openness to change is appropriate and other times when it may be disastrous. Organizations, in fact, should reward people who act as counterchange agents to create forces against the seduction of novelty for its own sake.

How can the leadership of these new style organizations create an atmosphere of continuity and stability amidst an environment of change? Whitehead put the problem well:

> The art of society consists first in the maintenance of the symbolic code, and secondly, in the fearlessness of revision . . . Those societies which cannot combine reverance to their symbols with freedom of revision must ultimately decay. . . .

There is no easy solution to the tension between stability and change. We are not yet an emotionally adaptive society, though we are as close to having to become one as any society in history. Elting Morison suggests in his brilliant essay on change that "we may find at least part of our salvation in identifying ourselves with the adaptive process and thus share some of the joy, exuberance, satisfaction, and security . . . to meet . . . changing times."

The remarkable aspect of our generation is its commitment to change in thought and action. Executive leadership must take some responsibility in creating a climate that provides the security to identify with the adaptive process without fear of losing status. Creating an environment that would increase a tolerance for ambiguity and where one can make a virtue out of contingency, rather than one that induces hesitancy and its reckless counter-part, expedience, is one of the most challenging tasks for the new leadership.

*Clarity, Commitment, and Consensus*

Organizations, like individuals, suffer from "identity crises." They are not only afflictions that attack during adolescence, but chronic states pervading every phase of organizational development. The new organizations we speak of, with their bands of professional problem-solvers, coping within a turbulent environment, are particularly allergic to problems of identity. Professional and regional orientations lead frequently to fragmentation, intergroup conflicts, and power plays and rigid compartmentalization, devoid of any unifying sense of purpose or mission.

The university is a wondrous place for advanced battle techniques, far surpassing their business counterparts in subterfuge and sabotage. Quite often a university becomes a loose collection of competing departments, schools, institutes, committees, centers, programs, largely noncommunicating because of the multiplicity of specialist jargons and interests, and held together, as Robert Hutchins once said, chiefly by a central heating system, or as Clark Kerr amended, by questions of what to do about the parking problem.

The modern organizations we speak of are composed of men who love independence as fiercely as the ancient Greeks; but it is also obvious that they resist what every Athenian, as a matter of course, gave time and effort for: "building and lifting up the common life."

Thucydides has Pericles saying:

We are a free democracy. . . . We do not allow absorption in our own affairs to interfere with participation in the city's. We regard men who hold aloof from public affairs as useless; nevertheless we yield to none in independence of spirit and complete self-reliance.

A modern version of the same problem (which the Greeks couldn't solve either, despite the lofty prose) has been stated by the president of a large university:

The problem with this institution is that too few people understand or care about the overall goals. Typically they see the world through their own myopic departmental glasses; i.e., too constricted and biased. What we need more of are professional staff who can wear not only their own school or departmental "hat" but the overall university hat.

Specialism, by definition, implies a peculiar slant, a skewed vision of reality. McLuhan tells a good joke on this subject. A tailor went to Rome and managed to get an audience with his Holiness. Upon his return, a friend asked him, "What did the Pope look like?" The tailor answered, "A 41 regular."

Having heard variations of this theme over the years, a number of faculty and administrators, who thought they could "wear the overall university hat" formed what later came to be known as "the HATS group." They came from a variety of departments and hierarchical levels and represented a rough microcosm of the entire university. The HATS group has continued to meet over the past several years and has played an important role in influencing university policy.

There are a number of functions that leadership can perform in addition to developing HATS groups. First, it can identify and support those persons who are "linking pins," individuals with a psychological and intellectual affinity for a number of languages and cultures. Secondly, it can work at the places where the different disciplines and organizations come together (for example, setting up new interdisciplinary programs), in order to create more intergroup give and take.

The third important function for leadership is developing and shaping identity. Organizations, not only the academic disciplines, require philosophers, individuals who can provide articulation between seemingly inimical interests, and who can break down the pseudospecies, transcend vested interests, regional ties, and professional biases. This is precisely what Mary Parker Follett had in mind when she discussed leadership in terms of an ability to bring about a "creative synthesis" between differing codes of conduct.

Chester Barnard in his classic *Functions of the Executive* (1938) recognized this, as well as the personal energy and cost of political process. He wrote, "it seems to me that the struggle to maintain cooperation among men should as surely destroy some men morally as battle destroys some physically."

### The Problem of Growth and Decay

For the leader, the organization has to take a conscious responsibility for its own evolution; without a planned methodology and explicit direction, the enterprise will not realize its full potential. For the leader, this is the issue of revitalization and it confronts him with the ultimate challenge: growth or decay.

The challenge for the leader is to develop a climate of inquiry and enough psychological and employment security for continual reassessment and renewal. This task is connected with the leader's ability to collect valid data, feed it back to the appropriate individuals, and develop action planning on the basis of the data. This three-step "action-research" model sounds deceptively simple. In fact, it is difficult. Quite often, the important data cannot be collected by the leader for many obvious reasons. Even when the data are known, there are many organizational short circuits and "dithering devices" that distort and prevent the data from getting to the right places at the right time. And even when data-gathering and feedback are satisfactorily completed, organizational inhibitions may not lead to implementation.

In response to the need for systematic data collection, many organizations are setting up "Institutional Research" centers that act as basic fact-gathering agencies. In some cases, they become an arm of policy-making. Mostly, they see as their prime responsibility the collection and analysis of data that bear on the effectiveness with which the organization achieves its goals.

Fact-gathering, by itself, is rarely sufficient to change attitudes and beliefs and to overcome natural inertia and unnatural resistance to change. Individuals have an awesome capacity to "selectively inattend" to facts that may in their eyes threaten their self-esteem. Facts and reason may be the least potent forms of influence that man possesses.

Some progressive organizations are setting up organizational development departments that attempt to reduce the "implementation gap" between information and new ideas and action. These OD departments become the center for the entire strategic side of the organization, including not only long-run planning, but plans for gaining participation and commitment to the plans. This last step is the most crucial for the guarantee of successful implementation.

In addition to substantive competence and comprehension of both social and technical systems, the new leader will have to possess interpersonal skills, not the least of which is the ability to defer his own immediate desires and gratifications in order to cultivate the talents of others. Let us examine some of the ways leadership can successfully cope with the new organizational patterns.

## Understanding the "social territory"

"You gotta know the territory," sang "Professor" Harold Hill to his fellow salesmen in *The Music Man.* The "social territory" encompasses the complex and dynamic interaction of individuals, roles, groups, organizational and cultural systems. Organizations are, of course, legal, political, technical, and economic systems. For our purposes, we will focus on the social system.

Analytic tools, drawn primarily from social psychology and sociology, are available to aid in the understanding of the social territory. But we need more than such tools to augment and implement these understandings. Leadership is as much craft as science. The main instrument or "tool" for the leader-as-a-craftsman is *himself* and how creatively he can use his own personality. This is particularly important for leaders to understand, for, like physicians, they are just as capable of spreading as of curing disease. And again, like the physician, it is important that the leader heed the injunction "heal thyself" so that he does not create pernicious effects unwittingly. Unless the leader understands his actions and effects on others, he may be a "carrier" rather than a solver of problems. Understanding the social territory and how one influences it is related to the "action-research" model of leadership mentioned earlier: 1) collect data, 2) feed it back to appropriate sources, and 3) action-planning. The "hang-up" in most organizations is that people tend to distort and suppress data for fear of real or fancied retaliation. (Samuel Goldwyn, a no-

torious martinet, called his top staff together after a particularly bad box-office flop and said: "Look, you guys, I want
you to tell me exactly what's wrong with this operation and
my leadership—even if it means losing your job!")

*The Concept of "System-Intervention"*

Another aspect of the social territory that has key sig-
nificance for leadership is the idea of *system*. At least
two decades of research have been making this point unsuccessfully. Research has shown that productivity can be
modified by what the group thinks important, that training
effects fade out and deteriorate if they do not fit the goals
of the social system, that group cohesiveness is a powerful
motivator, that conflict between units is a major problem
in organizations, that individuals take many of their cues
and derive a good deal of their satisfaction from their
primary work group, that identification with the small
work group turns out to be the only stable predictor of
productivity, and so on.

The fact that this evidence is so often cited and rarely
acted upon leads one to infer that there is some sort of
involuntary reflex that makes us locate problems in faulty
individuals rather than in malfunctioning social systems.
What this irrational reflex is based upon is not altogether
clear. But individuals, living amidst complex and subtle
organizational conditions, do tend to oversimplify and distort complex realities so that people rather than conditions
embody the problem. This tendency toward personalization can be observed in many situations. In international
affairs, we blame our troubles with France on deGaulle, or
talk sometimes as though we believe that replacing Diem,
or Khanh, or Ky will solve our problems with the Saigon
government. Other illustrations can be seen when members
of organizations take on familial nicknames, such as "Dad,"

"Big Brother," "Man," "Mother Hen," "Dutch Uncle," etc. We can see it in distorted polarizations such as the "good guy" leader who is too trusting, and his "hatchet man" assistant who is really to blame. These grotesques seem to bear such little resemblance to the actual people that one has to ask what psychological needs are being served by this complex labeling and stereotyping.

One answer was hinted at earlier in the Freud quote. He said that work provides an outlet for displacing emotional components onto professional work and the human relations associated with work. If there were no "Big Daddys" or "Queen Bees," we would have to invent them as therapeutic devices to allay anxieties about less romantic, more immediate mothers and fathers, brothers and sisters.

Another reason for this tendency toward personalization is related to the wounded narcissism leaders often suffer. Organizations are big, complex, wondrous—and hamstrung with inertia. Impotence and alienation imprison the best of men, the most glorious of intentions. There is a myth that the higher one goes up the ladder, the more freedom and potency one experiences. In fact, this is frequently not the case, as almost any chief executive will report: the higher he goes the more tethered and bound he may feel by expectations and commitments. In any case, as one gets entrapped by inertia and impotence, it is easier to blame heroes and villains than the system. For if the problems are embroidered into the fabric of the social system, complex as they are, the system can be changed. But if the problems are people, then the endemic lethargy can be explained away by the difficulty—the impossibility—of "changing human nature."

If management insists on personalizing problems that

arise from systems, serious repercussions must result. In the new organizations—where roles will be constantly changing and ambiguous, where changes in one subsystem will clearly affect other subsystems, where diverse activities have to be coordinated and integrated, where individuals work simultaneously in many different jobs and groups—a system viewpoint must be developed. Just as psychotherapists find it difficult to treat a "problem child" without treating the entire family, it will be more difficult to influence individual behavior without working with his particular subsystem. The leader will be compelled to intervene at the system level if the intervention is to last and serve its purpose.

## An Agricultural Model of Leadership

I have not found the right word or phrase that accurately portrays the concept of leadership I have in mind—which can be summarized as follows: *an active method for producing conditions where people and ideas and resources can be seeded, cultivated, and integrated to optimum effectiveness and growth.* The phrase "other-directedness," unfortunately, has taken on the negative tone of "exclusively tuned into outside cues." For awhile I thought that "applied biology" might capture the idea, for it connotes an ecological point of view; a process of observation, careful intervention, and organic development. I have also noticed that many biologists and physicians (particularly those physicians who either have no practices or went into public health, psychiatry, or research) are excellent administrators. Socrates used a close and congenial metaphor to symbolize the role of the teacher, the "midwife," someone who helped others to give birth to creations.

The most appropriate metaphor I have found to characterize adaptive leadership is an "agricultural" model.

The leader's job, as I have stated, is to build a climate where growth and development are culturally induced. Roy Ash, an astute industrialist and chairman of Litton Industries, remarked recently, "If the larger corporations, classically viewed as efficient machines rather than hothouses for fomenting innovation, can become both of these at once, industrial competition will have taken on new dimensions." I think Ash captures exactly the shift in metaphor I am getting at, from a mechanical model to an organic one. Up until very recent times, the metaphor most commonly used to describe power and leadership in organizations derived from Helmholtz's laws of mechanics. Max Weber, who first conceptualized the model of bureaucracy, wrote, "Bureaucracy is like a modern judge who is a vending machine into which the pleadings are inserted along with the fee and which then disgorges the judgment with its reasons mechanically derived from the code."

The language of organizational dynamics in most contemporary writings reflects the machine metaphor: social engineering, equilibrium, friction, resistance, force-field, etc. The vocabulary for adaptive organizations requires an organic metaphor, a description of a *process,* not structural arrangements. This process must include such terms as open, dynamic systems, developmental, organic, adaptive, etc.

All of these strategic and practical considerations lead to a totally new concept of leadership. The pivotal aspect of this concept is that it relies less on the leader's substantive knowledge about a particular topic than it does on the understanding and possession of skills summarized under the agricultural model.

This new concept of leadership embraces four important sets of competencies: 1) knowledge of large, complex human systems; 2) practical theories of intervening and guiding these systems, theories that encompass methods for seeding, nurturing, and integrating individuals and groups; 3) interpersonal competence, particularly the sensitivity to understand the effects of one's own behavior on others and how one's own personality shapes his particular leadership style and value system; and 4) a set of values and competencies which enables one to know when to confront and attack, if necessary, and when to support and provide the psychological safety so necessary for growth.

It is amusing and occasionally frustrating to note that the present view of leadership which I have referred to as an agricultural model, is often construed as "passive" or "weak" or "soft" or more popularly "permissive," and generally dismissed with the same uneasy, patronizing shrug one usually reserves for women who try, however clumsily, to play a man's game. The fact is that the role of leadership described here is clearly more demanding and formidable than any other historical precedent, from king to Pope.

It may be that the common tendency to give this new leadership role such passive and effeminate names betrays the anxiety that many must feel at the final downfall of that distant, stern, strict Victorian father, whose surrogate has led us so often as teacher, military commander, and corporation president. Perhaps that is the only kind of authority we have experienced first hand, or know intimately, or even consider legitimate. But if this new man of power —other-directed and interpersonally competent—takes over the dominant role, as he now seems to be doing, then not only will new myths and archetypes have to substitute for the old, family ones, but new ways—perhaps new legends—will have to be developed to dramatize the rise of new heroes. Let us hope that this new tradition of leadership is not only more potent, but in the long run more gratifying.

*July/August 1969*

## NOTES ON CONTRIBUTORS

Chris Argyris     "Being Human and Being Organized"

Professor of administrative sciences and member of the board of directors, Institute of Applied Social Science, Yale University. Argyris has been a consultant to the State Department, The National Institute of Mental Health and the Ford Foundation, as well as to business firms and European governments. His books include *Personality and Organization* and *Executive Leadership.*

Edward C. Devereux, Jr.     "Practical Problems and the Uses of Social Science"

Professor and chairman of the Department of Human Development and Family studies at Cornell University. Devereux has published papers on the sociology of deviant behavior, community participation, and family sociology. His current research is on cross-cultural studies of socialization.

William Gomberg     "The Trouble with Democratic Management"

Since 1959, professor of industry, Wharton School of Finance and Commerce, University of Pennsylvania. Gomberg has served as an arbitrator in the steel, automobile, electrical goods, textile, clothing and transportation industries. Recent publications are *Blue Collar World* (with Arthur Shostak) and *New Perspectives on Poverty* (with Arthur Shostak).

Alvin Gouldner     "Taking Over"

Max Weber Research Professor of Social Theory at Washington University, St. Louis. Gouldner's most recent book is *The Coming Crisis in Western Sociology.*

John T. Lanzetta     "The Innovating Organization: Innovation in Organizations"

Director of the Center for Research on Social Behavior at the University of Delaware.

Edward Emmett Lawler III     "How Much Money Do Executives Want"

Associate professor of administrative sciences and psychology at Yale University and director of undergraduate studies for the Administrative Sciences Department. Lawler's articles concerning management and organization structure have appeared in numerous professional journals.

Harold J. Leavitt    "The Innovating Organization: Ignorance, Success, and Innovation"

Professor of industrial administration and psychology at Carnegie Institute of Technology.

Abraham Maslow    "The Superior Person"

Professor of psychology at Brandeis University, currently on extended leave as resident fellow of the W. P. Laughlin Foundation in Menlo Park, California. Maslow is a past president of several professional societies including the American Psychological Association. His most recent book is *Motivation and Personality*.

Richard L. Meier    "The Innovating Organization: The Innovating Metropolis"

Research social scientist at the Mental Health Institute of the University of Michigan.

Robert K. Merton    "Practical Problems and the Uses of Social Science"

Giddings professor of sociology at Columbia University. Merton's paper, "Bureaucratic Structure and Personality" (1950) initiated research on the dysfunctions of bureaucracy. Later he co-authored and co-edited the first reader on bureaucracy (1952).

Donald C. Pelz    "The Innovating Organization: Conditions for Innovation"

Program director of the Survey Research Center of the University of Michigan, Pelz is currently working on analyses of scientific organization with Frank Andrews.

Ross Stagner    "Conflict in the Executive Suite"

Professor and chairman of the Department of Psychology at Wayne State University. Stagner's recent books include *Dimensions of Human Conflict* (1967) and *Basic Psychology* (1970).

Arthur Stinchcombe    "Organization-Creating Organizations"

In the Department of Social Relations at Johns Hopkins University.

Adolph Sturmthal    "Gray Flannel Unionist"

Since 1960 has been professor of labor and industrial relations at the University of Illinois. Among Sturmthal's books are *Workers*

*Councils: A Study of Workplace Organizations on Both Sides of the Iron Curtain* (1964) and *Current Manpower Problems* (1964). His edited volumes include *White Collar Trade Unions* (1966).

James Thompson      "The Innovating Organization: How to Prevent Innovation"

Professor of business administration at the Graduate School of Business of Indiana University.

Victor A. Thompson      How Scientific Management Thwarts Innovation"

Chairman of the department of political science at the University of Illinois. Thompson has studied how to make large formal organizations more innovative. His most recent book is *Bureaucracy and Innovation.*

James Q. Wilson      "The Innovating Organization: Necessity Versus the Devil"

Associate professor of government at Harvard.

John C. Wright      "The Innovating Organization: Curiosity and Opportunism"

Associate professor at the Institute of Child Development of the University of Minnesota.

# An Invitation To Subscribe To

## *trans*action

Social Science and Modern Society

*trans*action Magazine was the source for the articles of lasting interest presented in this book. *trans*action continuously publishes penetrating work of leading anthropologists, sociologists, psychologists, political scientists and economists. Keep in touch with the latest social research, including lively articles (like those in this book), summaries of important scientific findings, book reviews and illustrations by award-winning photographers and artists. Subscribe now to *trans*action at this special introductory rate:

*One full year of trans*action *Magazine for $6.00, a savings of $6.00 over the regular newsstand price and $2.50 over the yearly subscription price.*

---

YES, I would like to subscribe to *trans*action. I am enclosing $6.00 (check or money order) for the special introductory offer.

NAME

ADDRESS

City                        State            Zip Code

I would like to give *trans*action Magazine to a friend at the special introductory price of $6.00 (I am enclosing a check or money order). *trans*action will send a handsome card notifying them.

TO:                                  FROM:

NAME                               NAME

ADDRESS                          ADDRESS

City                                 City

State                               State

    Zip Code                       Zip Code

*trans*action, Box A, Rutgers, The State University, New Brunswick, N.J. 08903
Please use the back of this card for additional subscriptions.

# If You Had Been A Subscriber To
## *trans* action
# You Would Have Read:

The End of American Party Politics

The American Underclass: Red, White and Black *(special issue)*

White Gangs

Intelligence—Why it Grows, Why it Declines

Deviance and Democracy in San Francisco *(special issue)*

Roots of Black Manhood

Cuba Ten Years After *(special issue)*

The Brutality of Modern Families

Hard Core Unemployment

Dixie's New Left

Actors Search For a Self

Tearoom Trade: Impersonal Sex in Public Places

Religion and Politics in Northern Ireland

NAME

ADDRESS

City

State

Zip Code

NAME

ADDRESS

City

State

Zip Code

NAME

ADDRESS

City

State

Zip Code

NAME

ADDRESS

City

State

Zip Code

*trans*action, Box A, Rutgers, The State University, New Brunswick, N.J. 08903
Please use this card for additional subscriptions.